First World War
and Army of Occupation
War Diary
France, Belgium and Germany

41 DIVISION
Divisional Troops
Royal Army Service Corps
296 Company ASC
1 May 1916 - 30 September 1919

WO95/2631/3

The Naval & Military Press Ltd
www.nmarchive.com
Published in association with The National Archives

Published by

The Naval & Military Press Ltd

Unit 10 Ridgewood Industrial Park,

Uckfield, East Sussex,

TN22 5QE England

Tel: +44 (0) 1825 749494

www.naval-military-press.com

www.nmarchive.com

This diary has been reprinted in facsimile from the original. Any imperfections are inevitably reproduced and the quality may fall short of modern type and cartographic standards.

© **Crown Copyright**
Images reproduced by permission of The National Archives, London, England, 2015.

Contents

Document type	Place/Title	Date From	Date To
Heading	WO95/2631/3 296 Coy ASC		
Heading	BEF 41 Div Train 296 Coy ASC 1916 May-1917 Oct 1918 Mar-1919 Sept Italy 1917 Nov-1918 Feb		
War Diary	Aldershot	01/05/1916	01/05/1916
War Diary	Havre	02/05/1916	03/05/1916
War Diary	Strazeele	04/05/1916	26/05/1916
War Diary	La Creche	27/05/1916	20/08/1916
War Diary	Fletre	21/08/1916	24/08/1916
War Diary	Fletre & Long	24/08/1916	24/08/1916
War Diary	Long	25/08/1916	01/09/1916
War Diary	Argoeuves	02/09/1916	02/09/1916
War Diary	Buire	03/09/1916	10/09/1916
War Diary	Albert	11/09/1916	18/09/1916
War Diary	Buire	19/09/1916	23/09/1916
War Diary	Becordel	24/09/1916	31/10/1916
Miscellaneous	March Orders by Lieut Colonel W.W. Molony A.S.C.		
War Diary	Becordel	31/10/1916	31/10/1916
War Diary	Bonnay	01/11/1916	02/11/1916
War Diary	Villers Bocage	03/11/1916	03/11/1916
War Diary	Orville	04/11/1916	04/11/1916
War Diary	Monchel	05/11/1916	05/11/1916
War Diary	Anvin	06/11/1916	08/11/1916
War Diary	Molinghem	09/11/1916	09/11/1916
War Diary	Staple	10/11/1916	10/11/1916
War Diary	Reninghelst	11/11/1916	13/06/1917
War Diary	Ouderdom	14/06/1917	20/06/1917
War Diary	Zevcoten	21/06/1917	22/06/1917
War Diary	Renninghelst	23/06/1917	23/06/1917
War Diary	Zevcoten	24/06/1917	05/07/1917
War Diary	Schaexken	06/07/1917	21/07/1917
War Diary	Schaexken & Zevcoten	22/07/1917	22/07/1917
War Diary	Zevcoten	23/07/1917	02/09/1917
War Diary	Boeschepe	03/09/1917	11/09/1917
War Diary	Boeschepe & Zevcoten	12/09/1917	12/09/1917
War Diary	Zevcoten	13/09/1917	07/10/1917
War Diary	Zermezeele	08/10/1917	08/10/1917
War Diary	St. Pol. Sur Mare	09/10/1917	11/10/1917
War Diary	St. Pol.	12/10/1917	13/10/1917
War Diary	St. Idesbald	14/10/1917	28/10/1917
War Diary	Ghyvelde	29/10/1917	31/10/1917
War Diary	Valla	01/03/1918	04/03/1918
War Diary	Paese	05/03/1918	09/03/1918
War Diary	Doullens	13/03/1918	13/03/1918
War Diary	Beaurepaire	14/03/1918	20/03/1918
War Diary	Bavelincourt	21/03/1918	21/03/1918
War Diary	Achiet-Le-Petit	22/03/1918	24/03/1918
War Diary	St Amand	25/03/1918	25/03/1918
War Diary	Bailleulmont	26/03/1918	27/03/1918
War Diary	Humbercamp	28/03/1918	01/04/1918
War Diary	Henu	02/04/1918	12/04/1918

War Diary	Couin	13/04/1918	14/05/1918
War Diary	La. Lovie Chateau	15/05/1918	15/05/1918
War Diary	Leicester Camp	16/05/1918	17/05/1918
War Diary	Woods Area Leicester Camp	18/05/1918	18/05/1918
War Diary	Woods On Peselhoek-Woesten Rd.	19/05/1918	24/05/1918
War Diary	Woods Area Peselhoek Road.	25/05/1918	31/05/1918
War Diary	Woods W. Of Poperinge-Eykhoek Rd.	01/06/1918	05/06/1918
War Diary	Bambecque Area.	06/06/1918	06/06/1918
War Diary	Bollezeele Area.	07/06/1918	07/06/1918
War Diary	Ruminghem Area	08/06/1918	25/06/1918
War Diary	Steenvoorde Area	26/06/1918	30/06/1918
War Diary	Steenvoorde Area. Waton France Farm	05/07/1918	01/09/1918
War Diary	Near Abeele	02/09/1918	02/09/1918
War Diary	Abeele-Reninghelst. Road.	03/09/1918	03/09/1918
War Diary	Near Abeele	04/09/1918	07/09/1918
War Diary	Near Poperinghe	08/09/1918	19/09/1918
War Diary	Sheet 27 L34. C.4.6 Abeele Reninghelst Road	20/09/1918	20/09/1918
War Diary	Sheet 27 L34 C4.6	21/09/1918	26/09/1918
War Diary	Sheet 27 L 34 C 4.6 Abeele Reninghelst Rd.	27/09/1918	28/09/1918
War Diary	Brandhoek	29/09/1918	01/10/1918
War Diary	Voormezeele	02/10/1918	04/10/1918
War Diary	Belgian Battery Corner.	05/10/1918	12/10/1918
War Diary	Woodcote House. Sheet 28120. C 32.	13/10/1918	15/10/1918
War Diary	Dadizeele	16/10/1918	19/10/1918
War Diary	Near Gulleghem.	20/10/1918	20/10/1918
War Diary	Near Bisseghem	21/10/1918	22/10/1918
War Diary	Bisseghem	23/10/1918	28/10/1918
War Diary	Courtrai	29/10/1918	02/11/1918
War Diary	Courtrai Sweveghem Road	03/11/1918	04/11/1918
War Diary	Steenbrugge Area.	05/11/1918	06/11/1918
War Diary	Deerlyk Area.	07/11/1918	09/11/1918
War Diary	Ingoyghem. Area	10/11/1918	10/11/1918
War Diary	Schoorisse Area	11/11/1918	13/11/1918
War Diary	Nederbrakel	14/11/1918	17/11/1918
War Diary	Lust	18/11/1918	11/12/1918
War Diary	Viane.	12/12/1918	12/12/1918
War Diary	Tubize	13/12/1918	13/12/1918
War Diary	Briane-Le-Chateau	14/12/1918	15/12/1918
War Diary	Briane Le-L'Alleud	16/12/1918	16/12/1918
War Diary	Quatre Bras	17/12/1918	17/12/1918
War Diary	Eghezee	19/12/1918	19/12/1918
War Diary	Fumal	20/12/1918	21/12/1918
War Diary	Huy	22/12/1918	15/01/1919
War Diary	Germany Kalk	16/01/1919	20/01/1919
War Diary	Kalk	21/01/1919	30/09/1919

WO 95/2631/3

296 Coy ASC

BEF
41 Div Train

296 Coy ASC

1916 MAY — 1917 OCT
1918 MAR — 1919 SEPT
ITALY 1917 NOV — 1918 FEB

Army Form C. 2118

WAR DIARY or INTELLIGENCE SUMMARY
(Erase heading not required.)

HEAD QUARTERS COMPANY
DATE MAY 1916.
41st DIVISIONAL TRAIN.

Instructions regarding War Diaries and Intelligence Summaries are contained in F. S. Regs., Part II. and the Staff Manual respectively. Title Pages will be prepared in manuscript.

Place	Date	Hour	Summary of Events and Information	Remarks and references to Appendices
Aldershot	1/5/16		Entrained at Government Siding 2.20 p.m. & proceeded to Southampton. Entrained on S.S. Anselm. Shens (3) H.Q. horses changed by Vet. Offr at Southampton Dock, viz. Nos: 214, 231, & 155 & 3 H.D. horse issued, which were numbered 979, 980 & 981.	RQS
Havre	2/5/16		Disembarked at Havre at 9.20 A.M. & proceeded to rest Camp No. 2. No casualties.	RQS
Havre	3/5/16		Entrained at Havre at 7 p.m. Train leaving at 10 p.m.	RQS
Strazeele	4/5/16		Detrained at Steenbecque Station at 6.10 p.m. and proceeded to STRAZEELE by own march going into billets on arrival. Horses put on lines in field.	RQS
Strazeele	5/5/16		Passage injury rejoined Coy: Issued Sie & Pay Lt. Placed in/feing at HAZEBROUCK Gauge	RQS
Strazeele	6/5/16		Report of a piece selected on the STRAZEELE – MERRIS Road. Sgt. Sie & Lr	RQS
STRAZEELE	7/5/16		No.T4/94 Sgt. Dornton W.F. had his Coy arrested by his horse slipping on pave & falling with him. Sent to No.4 General Hospital. No. M3 Smith Fawcett H. attacked his Oye: Anema; ex. No.8 Ryde RFA Sent to hospital with Pneumonia.	RQS

WAR DIARY or INTELLIGENCE SUMMARY

(Erase heading not required.)

Army Form C. 2118

HEAD QUARTERS COMPANY
DATE MAY 1916
41st DIVISIONAL TRAIN.

Place	Date	Hour	Summary of Events and Information	Remarks and references to Appendices
STRAZEELE	8/5/16		Refitting as usual. O/c H.Q. Coy. gone sick with pneumonia.	MoD
Do:	9/5/16		Visited units of 103rd & 104th R.F.A Brigade.	MoD
Do:	10/5/16		Three (3) H.Q. Lorry sent to Mobile Veterinary Section at Borri, two suffering from sore withers, & one from strangles.	MoD
Do:	11/5/16		H.Q. Coy. with pneumonia much worse, Vet: Officer reports will not live.	MoD
Do:	12/5/16		H.Q. Coy. with pneumonia died & buried. Church of Strazeele by Revd. Order 429 dated 12/5/16. No: of horse 188	MoD
Do:	13/5/16		One (1) riding horse I.G: 20 set down & shot by Sgt: Palmalley, & knees badly broken, sent to Mobile Veterinary Section. One H.Q. Lorry, suffering from sore withers also sent to Mobile Vet: Sec: (No: 9). One (4) H.Q. Lorry received from Remount & transferred 26/5/16.	MoD
Do:	14/5/16		Stables, L.S.P., refitting as usual.	MoD
Do:	15/5/16		Inspected H.Q. Coy. Wagons & outfits & found all correct. H.Q. Lorry sent from Divide rejoins Sec: to Issue, Church of Strazeele from note 433	MoD
Do:	16/5/16		One school Franchie. Broke from Private E. Hadley, Driver of T.M. (Ovets on leave) posted to H.Q. Coy.	MoD

1875 Wt. W393/826 1,000,000 4/15 J.B.C. & A. A.D.S.S./Forms/C. 2118.

WAR DIARY or INTELLIGENCE SUMMARY

Army Form C. 2118

HEAD QUARTERS COMPANY
DATE: MAY 1916
41st DIVISIONAL TRAIN.

Place	Date	Hour	Summary of Events and Information	Remarks and references to Appendices
STRAZEELE	18/5/16		Divn Rodgr. A. Rankford to No. 2 Coy. & Dr. Russell T. Rankford fm No. 2 Coy to H.Q. Coy.	Ref?
Do.	19/5/16		Private Fawcett H. died at 18th Casualty Clearing Station (see Entry 17/5/16) See Train order 46.3 dated 20/5/16. Private Newell W. RASC R. Coy. 15th Hants Regt. joined at Kathen for Vet. Officer & posted to H.Q.Coy.	Ref?
Do.	19/5/16		Sergeant Robertson Rar to 140th Field Ambulance suffering from Shaven.	Ref?
Do.	20/5/16		Sergeant McKnight & Driver Steiner joined from 140th Field Ambulance. W/S J H.Q. horse, 1 riding horse & 1 mule to H.Q. Coy. Driver Fawcett struck off strength (see Entry dated 18/5/16). Driver Smith W.E. affected a/cty. L/Cpl. without pay. (Train order 4,5,6)	Ref?
Do.	21/5/16		Sergt: Rankin returned to duty fm 140th Field Ambulance (see Entry 19/5/16). Cpl: Sergt Sanders appointed acting Sergeant with pay (Train order 44.6). Sergt Butler T.N. with 1 riding horse & 1 mule fm 143rd Field Ambulance signed on Poss'n & taken on Strength Listing (Train order 46.7). Sergeant Matthews R. Foster, 1 HQ horse, 1 L.D. horse & 1 riding horse from 122nd Field Ambulance joined & taken on Strength Listing. (Train order 46.7)	Ref?
Do.	20/5/16		Major John D.A.C. signed H.Q. Coy. Lendgn Giles of Vgy L.G. C.O. from Junction to ride when to go on duty Quitrant Lerris A. Empans	Ref?

1875 Wt. W593/826 1,000,000 4/15 J.B.C. & A.   A.D.S.S./Forms/C.2118.

WAR DIARY
or
INTELLIGENCE SUMMARY

Army Form C. 2118

HEAD QUARTERS COMPANY
DATE MAY 1916
41st DIVISIONAL TRAIN

Place	Date	Hour	Summary of Events and Information	Remarks and references to Appendices
STRAZEELE	23/5/16		Isolation Sec. & I.S.C. Divn. Supply Co. attached from 1893 Field Ambulance.	
Do:	24/5/16		S. draught Horse & D. wagon from the 3 Field Ambulance sent to start Remount at Bailleul. CAESTRE as supply rail establishment. 4 G.S. wgn Cav & H + 4 ankle sets of P.D.O.S. horses handed to R.T.O. at CAESTRE in return for equal no of Surplus to establishment on the re-distribution of Pyles: Amm: Col: & Divn. Amm: Col. Reynolds, Leffingham, Andrews & Merrilees to Attenborough, T.W. & Divn. Supply Coln, Foster, Skinner, North, Williams & Carlisle transferred to base as surplus to establishments handed over to the R.T.O. at CAESTRE. All artillery supply wgn despatched to join their units at 6.30 p.m.	
Do:	25/5/16		M.H.D. Loves Staff & Middle Veterinary Section Waggon No: 121. Came in near Goddes last night. Dump attd to the STRAZEELE – MOLENACKER Rd.	
Do:	26/5/16		H.Q. Company marched from STRAZEELE to LA CRECHE by march route, arriving at Approving at 1.15 p.m. No casualties. Supply Section & Pack refilled at STRAZEELE ... LA CRECHE in advance.	

Army Form C. 2118

WAR DIARY
or
INTELLIGENCE SUMMARY
(Erase heading not required.)

HEAD QUARTERS COMPANY
DATE MAY 1916
41st DIVISIONAL TRAIN.

Place	Date	Hour	Summary of Events and Information	Remarks and references to Appendices
LA CRECHE	27/5/16		Picked at dump to Steenwerck Platm. — STEENWERCK — at) P.H. all Salvtables. Unit hire of Platms. D.A.D.T. 4th Army. A/Sgt. H.Q. 2/4 Lancs. Transport Platm. Party with the 208th attached to 122 Regt. Steenwerck. Brigade	Paul
Do	28/5/16		On scale, attached to P.D.2 Engr. now completed to shelter. Dug 2nd Sgt. Refuge from started to erect dining shed for O.R.M. Also weather? Sgmt. Whole shed finished at 1.5 A.M. No pr. B.head done. Site fine & fiat	Paul
Do	29/5/16		Late to time hard of any sign of running of placed to for a sale for Lance Cpls. Slight signs of progress at 4.5 depth. Dining shed for O.R.M. completed. On: Wade returned to duty h.k. No ? D Coy.	Paul
Do	30/5/16		Divn. H.Q.'s Arrived at La Creche. Weather fine	Paul
Do	31/5/16		Weather fine & W.	Paul
Do	1/6/16		Started to get of outskirts — STEENWERCK Platm — with Lyre transport wgn. Div. Supply Column. MMG & limber attached to their Batts. Arm. as shown. 187 Rgft. RFA. 142 Bde. RFA. 133 Bde. 2f. No. 2 by. 130 Rgft RFA 126 Feld Amm. 126 No. 2 by. 130 Rgft RFA 140? Field Amm. 3 k No. 4 Coy. 202 field Amm?	Paul

WAR DIARY or INTELLIGENCE SUMMARY

Army Form C. 2118

Place	Date	Hour	Summary of Events and Information	Remarks and references to Appendices
L.A CRECHE	2/6/16		Refilling at station as usual. Walker one night to Stonyhurst at G.O.C. visited lines in slightly modified outline.	
Do.	3/6/16		Dr. Alexander 2nd i/c Field Ambulance. Officers rich on lunch; our Sergt - Walker one.	
Do.	4/6/16		2 baggage wagons sent to No 7 RFA Bgde H.Q. to assist me with Signal Adv. as night being already with them. One bgde sent to Engineer ladder. Those hypt sent out bell lines + lines & shifted as required.	
Do.	5/6/16		Dr. Evans H. admitted to 158 Field Ambulance (sick). Lethe one. Dr. Symington EA transferred from No. 2 by Q. Bg. & for J. Spiers ASR from H.Q. & No 2 Eng.	
Do.	6/6/16		Dr. Deméré F. admitted to 188 Field ambulance (sick). Set in convoy. S/C. Roberts transferred to No 2 by & Sgt Chunchill from No 2 by to HQ Eng.	
Do.	7/6/16		Routine as usual.	

WAR DIARY
or
INTELLIGENCE SUMMARY

(Erase heading not required.)

Army Form C. 2118

HEAD QUARTERS COMPANY
41st DIVISIONAL TRAIN.

Place	Date	Hour	Summary of Events and Information	Remarks and references to Appendices
La Crèche	8/6/16		Sgt. Walker posted to H.Q. Coy. to replace a driver evacuated. Sgt Grant admitted 138th Field Ambulance sick. Sgt.	
Do.	9/6/16		Sgt. Alexander evacuated to Casualty Clearing Station, suffering from sick. 1 HQ late attached to Coy. evacuated, 3 other HQ Coy. evacuated.	
Do.	10/6/16		Considerable shelling of railway ahead to 2 a.m. & at dumps to 8.15 a.m. Enemy aircraft bombing convoys. Artillery Bde. & MTO's Building somewhat quieter during evening.	
Do.	11/6/16		Routine as usual. 1 HQ horse received from Remounts & attached to No. 2 Company.	
Do.	12/6/16		Sgt. Grant & Pannell returned to duty from 138th Field Ambulance. 1 SR	
Do.	13/6/16		Pte. Theodros admitted to 188th Field Ambulance suffering from ICT. 1 sick.	
Do.	14/6/16		Official time advanced one hour from 11 P.M. 1 SR	
Do.	15/6/16		1 heavy draught horse sent to Mobile Vet. Sec. Vig. No: 194 No Crim. suffering from Quittor.	

WAR DIARY
or
INTELLIGENCE SUMMARY
(Erase heading not required.)

Army Form C. 2118

HEAD QUARTERS COMPANY
DATE
No.
41st DIVISIONAL TRAIN.

Instructions regarding War Diaries and Intelligence Summaries are contained in F. S. Regs., Part II. and the Staff Manual respectively. Title Pages will be prepared in manuscript.

Place	Date	Hour	Summary of Events and Information	Remarks and references to Appendices
LA CRÈCHE	16/6/16		Routine as usual. Fine. 1 H.D. Lce Sergt. Inglis K.C. Sec: No: 166 Gaffney 1 H.S. Vet No: 151 Evacuated for duty to Base of Mech. Vet & Neuendi.	1 SgD
do.	17/6/16		Gas alarm in night 16/17th. One for Sickness. Fine. Tr.Vet. S.A. admitted to hospital sick. Brought Co. attacked by Leeches admitted to hospital sick. Incised with Acetic Acid.	1 SgD
do.	18/6/16		1 H.D. Lce Cpl Co/A.V.S. (No: 255) Lazard Brought from Field hospital sick. Sent down in Ambce 12/16 do. Sgt. Tr.Vet. "B" transferred hospital sick. Sent down Ambce. Qm. Ch. Sanders Discharged from hospital.	1 SgD
do.	19/6/16		Fine. Tr.Vet. C. discharged from hospital.	1 SgD
do.	20/6/16		Ors: Gray 18th disc discharged from hospital 2 H.D. Lapp evacuated to Base. Nos: 165-166 + DSS. Riding horses H.D. Hoggy Sent to 1234+134 Bgde Auxlre Ammn Sectus. Together with Harness + W.C.O's Saddling.	1 SgD
do.	21/6/16		Routine as Usual.	1 SgD

Army Form C. 2118

WAR DIARY
or
INTELLIGENCE SUMMARY
(Erase heading not required.)

Instructions regarding War Diaries and Intelligence Summaries are contained in F. S. Regs., Part II. and the Staff Manual respectively. Title Pages will be prepared in manuscript.

HEADQUARTERS COMPANY
DATE
No.
4TH DIVISIONAL TRAIN

Place	Date	Hour	Summary of Events and Information	Remarks and references to Appendices
LA CRECHE	22/6/16		Routine observed	[sig]
Do.	23/6/16		Dr: Searight – attached to No. 2 Coy. – transferred to base.	[sig]
Do.	24/6/16		Dr: Joseph, joined our reinforcement, attached to Dr. Bradley, graded special Llinor. Set. 20/6/16.	[sig]
Do.	25/6/16		2 HQ horses sent to Mule Vet. Sec. Vig. Nos. 277 & 177 suffering from debility & itch or Grease. 1 HQ horse attached to No.3 Coy. Sgt.15 M.V.S. with debility. Vig. No. 110.	[sig]
Do.	26/6/16		Dr: Snowden T. (conductor orderly) transferred to No. 2 Coy.	[sig]
Do.	27/6/16		Dr: Reuter attached No. 2 Coy. from H.Q. Coy. Admitted to hospital. Martin Pvt. No. 2 Coy. detailed to replace him.	[sig]

WAR DIARY or INTELLIGENCE SUMMARY

Army Form C. 2118

HEAD QUARTERS COMPANY
41st DIVISIONAL TRAIN

Place	Date	Hour	Summary of Events and Information	Remarks and references to Appendices
LA CRÊCHE	28/6/16		Routine as usual.	
Do.	29/6/16		Supplies refill; the 2nd refill being flour at 8 P.M. & unloading of frozen carcases from Supply Column.	
Do.	30/6/16		To refill at dump. Ration convoy held up awhile by civil: traffic. Return via FLÊTRE.	

WAR DIARY
or
INTELLIGENCE SUMMARY

(Erase heading not required.)

Army Form C. 2118

Instructions regarding War Diaries and Intelligence Summaries are contained in F.S. Regs., Part II. and the Staff Manual respectively. Title Pages will be prepared in manuscript.

HEAD QUARTERS COMPANY
DATE............
No..............
41st DIVISIONAL TRAIN

Place	Date	Hour	Summary of Events and Information	Remarks and references to Appendices
LA CRECHE	1/7/16		2 H.Q. Lorries, Nos. 110 & 277 travelled to base at 25/6/16 & struck off strength. 1 H.Q. Lorrie destroyed at Mil. Vet. Sec. No. 27/6/16 & struck off. M.T. Driver attached No. 2 Coys invalided to Church St. Straights 27/6/16. Orderly have received from D.A.S.	NoR
Do.	2/7/16		Dr. Rathee admitted to 138 Field Ambulance. Suffered pain	NoR
Do.	3/7/16		Routine as usual	NoR
Do.	4/7/16		1 H.Q. Lorrie No. 280 sent to Mil. Vet. Sec. On myps.	NoR
Do.	5/7/16		Routine as usual.	NoR
Do.	6/7/16		Dr. Birkenhead admitted 138 Field Ambulance. Injured Ryls. Set. Taylor W.O. admitted Staff Sergt	NoR

WAR DIARY
or
INTELLIGENCE SUMMARY
(Erase heading not required.)

Army Form C. 2118

HEAD QUARTERS COMPANY

41st DIVISIONAL TRAIN.

Place	Date	Hour	Summary of Events and Information	Remarks and references to Appendices
LA CRÈCHE	7/7/16		2 drivers & 1 Saddler driver from Base Horse Transport depot joined to this Coy. Dr. Crabtree C. wounded & base a 2.5 inst:	App 8
Do:	8/5/16		Routine as Usual	App 8
Do:	9/7/16		Empl Chr of all horses by O.C. Train.	App 84
Do:	10/7/16		Horse No: 280 evacuated to base (H.D.) Lee/Cpl Clarke reverted to driver at own request & transferred to H.Q 2/5 Army as a Batman	Do
Do:	11/7/16		Billing at Ouldread And found the S.A.M. ga this dury only	App 8
Do:	12/7/16		L/Cpl Crysele attended acting Cpl: vice Sergt Dr: Wilson G.A returned to duty from 138 F.A.	App. 8.
Do:	13/7/16		Routine as Usual	App 8

WAR DIARY
or
INTELLIGENCE SUMMARY

Army Form C. 2118

HEADQUARTERS COMPANY
41st DIVISIONAL TRAIN

Place	Date	Hour	Summary of Events and Information	Remarks and references to Appendices
LA CRÈCHE	14/7/16		Field Coy No. 2609 1 Offr & 2 privates attached to Coy. for supplies of 2nd Cavalry Division.	
Do.	15/7/16		Ors: 2. W. Cage to England. 1 H.S. Horse, 1 G.S. +1 limbered wagon (waggon) supplying Civil nursing Church of England. Available A.A. & Q.M.G. 41st Div. 2000 until 21/7/16	
Do.	16/7/16		Routine as Normal.	
Do.	17/7/16		7 H.S. limber No. 29 Sent to Supply for Sec. 4 G.S. Wggn & 4 H.S. Limb. 4 for drivers & 4 Loaders attached to Coy. from 20th Rifle & Infty Regt	
Do.	18/7/16		Routine as Normal	
Do.	19/7/16		Dr. Admual Sheaved by S.S. E. E. Slater. Sr. St. Kearsh Sr. West ed to hosp das Cult. Lush Church St. N.S. Rifle No: 29 Wounded to hosp & Church Kt Sheigh	
Do.	20/5/16		2 G.S. Wggn & H.S. Lorry & 8 ASC driver (waggons) for Supplies civ. Cavalry Church England as per 20/5/16 H.S. Lorry No. 246. H.S. Lorry No. 246 - attached No. 3 Bgd. deployed.	

WAR DIARY
or
INTELLIGENCE SUMMARY

(Erase heading not required.)

Army Form C. 2118

HEAD QUARTERS COMPANY
DATE
No.
41st DIVISIONAL TRAIN

Place	Date	Hour	Summary of Events and Information	Remarks and references to Appendices
LA CRECHE	21/7/16		Saddler Sergt: Graham S. afforded Staff Sergt. without pay	Aust
Do.	22/7/16		Routine as usual.	App
Do.	23/7/16		Routine as usual. Zepplin at Southend killed 5. 7.20 A.M.	App
Do.	24/7/16		Shelling at 2.30 mgr. Lt. D.S. Smith Hampstead & No. 2 Coy. 222 L.H. Nos. 5. No. 1 Coy. + 2216 H.L. Holland from No. 4 Coy. 14 Q Coy.	App
Do.	25/7/16		Sgt. Fennell & Arensford 583 Rostalle & Segrep Dr. Jennings C. from Sayl & No. 1 & Dy & A No. 2 Coy E.14 Q Coy. Remaining as usual.	App
Do.	26/7/16		Arriving as usual till Aerline as usual	App
Do.	27/7/16		Capts Pegg - Seabrook - Stiles; Eng; & Smith attached for supplies. Stilitt & Greely Larkin - Wale for Amm. Column.	App
Do.	28/7/16		Routine as usual	App

WAR DIARY
or
INTELLIGENCE SUMMARY

(Erase heading not required.)

Army Form C. 2118

HEAD QUARTERS COMPANY
DATE
No.
41st DIVISIONAL TRAIN.

Place	Date	Hour	Summary of Events and Information	Remarks and references to Appendices
LA CRÈCHE	29/6/16		One A.S.C. Lorry - No. 181 To No. 3 Coy. to replace one destroyed.	Ross
Do.	30/6/16		Routine as usual.	Ross
Do.	1/7/16		2 A.S.C. Lorries attached R.E. at ARMENTIÈRES killed by Shell fire. One & 1 G.S. Wagon destroyed 03:05 by W.E.	Ross

M.B. Parker Capt.
O.C. Hq. Qrs. Coy. 41st Divl. Train.

WAR DIARY or INTELLIGENCE SUMMARY

Army Form C. 2118

HEADQUARTERS COMPANY
41st DIVISIONAL TRAIN

Place	Date	Hour	Summary of Events and Information	Remarks and references to Appendices
LA CRÈCHE	1/8/16		Routine as usual. Viz:- Reveille 4 A.M. Stables 4-30 to 5-30. Breakfast 5-30. Guards & Supply etc.: to all at rulhead 6-30. Billeting at rulhead 7 A.M. Helped by dump. Refilling at dump. Artillery Stably 11 to 12. Gunners 12. Evening Stably 9-15 A.M. 3-30 to 6. Tea 6. Dinner 7. Call to lights 3-30 to 6. Guard On mule 5-45. Roll call & lights out 9 P.M. Water line 9 P.M.	RS
Do.	2/8/16		Routine as usual. All ranks in vicinity dry. Stables sealing letter of sympathy, Lord R. to SAILLEZ – ARMENTIÈRES road. RS	RS
Do.	3/8/16		Routine as usual. + G.S. wgn & water, + driveys & escorty attached from HQ to Stably return Laillebaie on 2/8/16 damaged on 2/8/16 returned to their unit. Infantry S/Sgt Inspector A.D.S. of train STEENWERCK. 2nd Lt. HOLLARD admitted to 138th Field Ambulance on 14/7/16 broke down, & replaced by Lovy No: 8732 THORNEY CROFT (4.S.)	RS
Note on 2/8/16 Lowy attached on 14/7/16 broke down, & replaced by Lovy No: 8732 THORNEY CROFT (4.S.)				

WAR DIARY
or
INTELLIGENCE SUMMARY

(Erase heading not required.)

Army Form C. 2118

HEAD QUARTERS COMPANY

41st Division

Place	Date	Hour	Summary of Events and Information	Remarks and references to Appendices
LA CRECHE	4/7/16		Routine as usual. Stretcher bearers of R.S.M. [illegible] Long & 2 dirties attached on 27/7/16 for supplies [illegible] (SB) & Gnr. [illegible] Gunn [illegible] Dunford [illegible] Pickett [illegible] Simpson Ratcliffe returned to unit.	
Do	5/7/16		2/Lt. HOLLARD evacuated to base. attached to 63rd Aust. Vet. Sec. in place of 2/Lt. WATKINS S.J. No. 79/1580 CARLING H. No. 70942 [illegible] Thorneycroft Long & 1 NCO & 1 private attached for duty. Sgt. [illegible] Suttle J. E. Notting [illegible] [illegible] Div. supply col. One in place of [illegible] Supr's Cox [illegible] Nurse Arthur G. N.Z. Lieut Stevens (attached to SD) & D attached to C+ (SD) Lines & trucks inspected by D.S.R. (MKi Herne Bay exchange ward Omaha) [illegible]	
Do	6/6/16		No. 74004 Dr. ATTEWELL A.J. sick 120 Light Machine gun Coy. dispatched on 28/7/16. 5.8 Carmody cleaning station & struck off [illegible] Luther [illegible]	

1875 Wt. W593/826 1,000,000 4/15 J.B.C. & A. A.D.S.S./Forms/C.2118.

Army Form C. 2118

HEAD QUARTERS COMPANY
DATE........
No........
41st DIVISIONAL TRAIN

WAR DIARY
or
INTELLIGENCE SUMMARY
(Erase heading not required.)

Instructions regarding War Diaries and Intelligence Summaries are contained in F. S. Regs., Part II. and the Staff Manual respectively. Title Pages will be prepared in manuscript.

Place	Date	Hour	Summary of Events and Information	Remarks and references to Appendices
LA CRECHE	7/8/16		This A.S.C. personnel transferred by Nos 40372 transferred to No 2 Coy & Staffe set C.S. G.S. transfer - from 41 D. Train - Nos 109 & 113. Transferred to 4 Coy - full transfer to duty (reinforcements) namely Nos 101 Horse Rate depot: Dvr T334 Dvr FROGGATT A.W.J., T4039 Dvr MALLETT H.R. T4354 Dvr GODWIN A, T4502 Dvr MARSHALL R, T/35065 T/35067 Dvr MITTEN J, T/35068 Dvr MARSH H, etc weather fine.	(Sgd)
Do.	8/8/16		1 A.S.C. horse attached to No. 2 Coy. Evacuated sick to hosp: 1 O.Rank of strength. 1 A.S. horse No. 112 sent to extra sty. weather fine.	(Sgd)
Do.	9/8/16		Routine of work. Weather fine & fair	(Sgd)

1875 Wt. W593/826 1,000,000 4/15 J.B.C. & A. A.D.S.S./Forms/C. 2118.

Army Form C. 2118

WAR DIARY
or
INTELLIGENCE SUMMARY
(Erase heading not required.)

HEAD QUARTERS COMPANY
41st Divisional Train

Place	Date	Hour	Summary of Events and Information	Remarks and references to Appendices
LA CRÈCHE	10/8/16		Routine as Usual. Brother Gun & Coll.	MSL
Do.	11/8/16		Routine as Usual. Brother Gun & Coll.	PSL
Do.	12/8/16		L/Cde. No. 20. Coy for Vice & Supt to 59th Inf Bde. Vet Section Brother Gun shell. Received G.S. Lyth from A.O.D. to replace one damaged by shell fire & for Brother Gun & Coll. 30/7/16.	PSL
Do.	13/8/16		Routine as Usual. Brother Gun.	PSL
Do.	14/8/16		Gun O. refilling allotted to 9.45 AM. No. 74/233 No. 02/5/33. Ammn Dump Refilling. Dr. COLE. F. admitted to 138 Fd. Ambces. The Bury aby The Roy Aniltry Pnk. Field Ambulance. Rain in morning; rain in afternoon.	PSL
Do.	15/8/16		No: 74508 Dr: WILSON J.F. admitted 136 Fd Field Ambulance Routine as Usual. RFA suffg. & Inflamn lung. Bro Gun 8 Coll.	PSL

WAR DIARY or INTELLIGENCE SUMMARY

Army Form C. 2118

HEAD QUARTERS COMPANY
41st DIVISIONAL TRAIN

Place	Date	Hour	Summary of Events and Information	Remarks and references to Appendices
LA CRECHE	16/8/16		No. T4/066/200 Pte. COLE.F. discharged from 138th Field Ambulance. 1 riding horse received from D.A.C. 11 Recruits received from Remounts CAESTRE. R.S.A. supply & baggage wagons attached from 1st Corps Siege Bty. R.S.A. supply & baggage wagons attached from 108 Siege Bty. Drawing rations in FLETRE	A.B.
Do.	17/8/16		Train H.Q.S. left FLETRE.	A.B.
Do.	18/8/16		All R.F.A. & D.A.C. baggage wagons detached to their units. [signed]	A.B.
Do.	19/8/16		Rations drawn in Ouderdom. [signed] No.T4/066/202 Pte. Wilson J.F. discharged from 138th Field Ambulance	A.B.
Do.	20/8/16		H.Q. Company ordered to LA CRECHE to FLETRE arriving 1.15 P.M. by march order. Unloading at 10.30 A.M. & moving over camp at LA CRECHE to refilling point. Place A.Q. Eng. 232nd Div. Train Refilling point CAESTRE. Fine.	A.B.

WAR DIARY or INTELLIGENCE SUMMARY

Army Form C. 2118

HEAD QUARTERS COMPANY
41st DIVISIONAL TRAIN

Place	Date	Hour	Summary of Events and Information	Remarks and references to Appendices
FLETRE	21/8/16		Refilling CAESTRE at 10 A.M. Capt. R.E.M.P. proceeded to REMY to arrange billets, leaving BAILLEUL at 6.20 P.M. 1H.D, 2H.D, & L.D. Lorry & 1 Motor Cycle received from Remounts. 2 H.D. Drivers Grundels received from remounts as spares for supplies. Heavy rain & thunder storm in night. $\frac{Q}{Q}$ 21/8/16	158
do.	22/8/16		Routine as usual. Spare cycle in ongoing for certain titles ?R.F.A. Unit left here. My Day Supplies Coy. 3. L.D. lorries issued to 15. 1405 Field Ambulance. 15. 265 Hopkins 15. 123 Pigg H.Q. Spare cycle still in use by R.F.A.	BR
do.	23/8/16		Spare cycle still in use of R.F.A. Rather fine.	BR
do.	24/8/16		H.Q. Train & H.Q. Coy left FLETRE at 7 A.M. & proceeded to BAILLEUL, gas (West) arriving there 3.10 A.M. Entrained at Rly. Station. Train left 6.18 A.M. & proceeded to PONT REMY. Arrived there 3.45 P.M. Detrained & proceeded to Church (extract on next sheet)	

WAR DIARY or INTELLIGENCE SUMMARY

Army Form C. 2118

HEAD QUARTERS COMPANY
41st DIVISION

Place	Date	Hour	Summary of Events and Information	Remarks and references to Appendices
FLETRE & LONG.			(Continuation from previous page.) to LONG, arriving there at 7 P.M. Reported at PONT REMY Station. Wire No. 4/4 094/152 Or: FEARIS N. Led the Train from a high truck on the line, refused same to R.T.O. who told her Rn. R.T.O. PONT REMY Commandant in Station or the line. Telegram received at 11.25 to an effect that Or: FEARIS had ten seriously injured, losing the Sgt & two thirds of their foot & had been admitted to No. 13 General Hospital. Referred same to H.Q. Rouen. A line visited by Camp Commandant (enps) all satisfactory, weather fine flying critic. Splendid. Weather fine.	[Ms.]
LONG	26/6/16		Refitting Dark on ground about 1 mile S.E. LONG. Horse lines kind to Camp Commandant (enps) all satisfactory, weather fine flying phase is in vogue. No. 4 094/152 Or: FEARIS N. Struck by sleepers.	[Ms.]

WAR DIARY or INTELLIGENCE SUMMARY

Army Form C. 2118

HEADQUARTERS COMPANY
41st DIVISIONAL TRAIN

Place	Date	Hour	Summary of Events and Information	Remarks and references to Appendices
LONG.	26/6/16		Refilling at LONG – PONT REMY and later 2½ Only from LONG. at 9 A.M. No.74/843500 Dr WADE.W. & No.74/843383 Dr GILDART.J. admitted to No.15 Field Ambulance. No.74/294236 Dr. BARRET.F. who admitted to No.15 Field Ambulance. Sgn. H.Q. Coy. & No.3 Coy. acting Lce Kauffmuch Weather fine.	PSN
Do.	27/6/16		Refilling as Usual. Weather fine.	PSN
Do.	28/6/16		Refilling as Usual. Weather showery	PSN
Do.	29/6/16		No.73/22790 Dr ALDRIDGE.H.J. admitted to No.15 Field Ambulance. Weather wet & Stormy. Refilling as Usual	PSN
Do.	30/6/16		Refilling as Usual. Very wet. Men sleeping in bivouacs carried to building adjoining Coy Office in Village on account of wet ground	PSN

Army Form C. 2118

WAR DIARY
or
INTELLIGENCE SUMMARY

(Erase heading not required.)

Instructions regarding War Diaries and Intelligence Summaries are contained in F.S. Regs., Part II. and the Staff Manual respectively. Title Pages will be prepared in manuscript.

HEADQUARTERS COMPANY
41st DIVISIONAL TRAIN.

Place	Date	Hour	Summary of Events and Information	Remarks and references to Appendices
LONG	31/8/16		Routine as usual. No. T/2/4017 D/Sgt. BEACH. J. & T/SR.02179 Dr. SMITH. S.J. admitted 136th Field Ambulance suffering from Kicks, Scratches &c.	P.S.O.

M.B. Barker Capt
O.C. Hd. Qrs. Coy. 41st Divl. Train.

WAR DIARY
or
INTELLIGENCE SUMMARY

Army Form C. 2118

Place	Date	Hour	Summary of Events and Information	Remarks and references to Appendices
LONG.	1/9/16.		Morning section on Supply duties so Nos. 344 & 345 were being inspected by O.C. Train. All transport began start to unit at 4 p.m. Supply section & Supply Vehicle left LONG at 6.30 p.m. & proceeded to ARGOEUVES & arrived the Supply Vehicle being handed over to their unit & cooks. Armed ARGOEUVES at 4.30 A.M. 2/9/16.	[sgd]
ARGOEUVES	2/9/16.		Supply section refilled at AILLY at 10 A.M. began remaining with their units. H.Q. Coy. left ARGOEUVES at 9.30 p.m. proceeding to a camping ground close to BUIRE arriving there at 6-15 A.M. 3/9/16. all Supply & Baggage Vehicles travelled with their unit. Isothen Coy. No. 73 Dr ALDRIDGE H.T. & No. 7500 Dr. WADE W. Evacuated from Field Ambulance to No. 2/27790 5 [?] 43-500 Stationary Hospital & Struck off the Strength 2/9/16.	[sgd]
BUIRE.	3/9/16.		Supply refilled at 10 A.M. & at 2 P.M. in roadside of road leading from BERNANCOURT to on any AMIENS - ALBERT good, all supply Vehicles remaining with their units. Rain in afternoon. [Continued on next page]	[sgd]

WAR DIARY
or
INTELLIGENCE SUMMARY

(Erase heading not required.)

Army Form C. 2118

HEADQUARTERS COMPANY
DATE
No.
41st DIVISIONAL TRAIN

Place	Date	Hour	Summary of Events and Information	Remarks and references to Appendices
BUIRE	3/9/16		Continued Run carrying. The undermentioned off. & other ranks enlisted in Siam. Orders 2/9/16. No. M2/162969 Private GOWER. A.D. is to Acting L/Cpl. Acting Cpl. M2/033111 " EARDLEY. W. " " M2/46157 " TAIT. J.J " "	Rd
Do.	4/9/16		Refilling at 2.45 P.M. On a time split as in 3rd inst: O.C 62 of M.V.S. to take a Church Sce Sleigh in Lorum Ohio. 3rd inst. O.C Train Rifled Church Army Parade Slarry	Rd
Do.	5/9/16		Refilling at 4 P.M. on Same split as a 3rd inst. Route Slarry	Rd
Do.	6/9/16		Refilling at 1.30 P.M. on 7th East Branch & Coord ends Rds. on BUIRE-Clippet to Amiens-Albert Road. No.Ty/784 Dr. KING. D.H. admitted D.T.C Field Ambulance sick. Route time	Rd

WAR DIARY
or
INTELLIGENCE SUMMARY

(Erase heading not required.)

Army Form C. 2118

HEADQUARTERS COMPANY
41st DIVISIONAL TRAIN

Place	Date	Hour	Summary of Events and Information	Remarks and references to Appendices
BUIRE	7/10/16		Refilling at R.H. Same spot as 6.5 Inf. No T4935 Dr. GILBART J. & No. T4236 Dr. BARRETT F. rejoined Coy. from No. 2 Coy Having been discharged from 140th Field Ambulance & 4th Inf: Brooke Amb.	RS
Do.	8/10/16		Refilling at 1.20pm. Same spot as 6.5 Inf: No T WST Sgt. BEACH J. discharged from Hospital & returned to duty. from 2nd/2nd Sthn: Genl. Amb.	RS
Do.	9/10/16		Same as usual.) H.Q. Lce No: 247 Pte L 59 ad Mobile Vet: Sec: evacuated to Church St Hosp.h No T4114 Dr. KING D.H. discharged from 21st Field Ambulance & rejoined Coy. No T 05129 SMITH S.O. Church St Hosp.K. Isola. Fre	RS
	10/9/16		No refill. 2 H.Q. horses No: 268 & 269 sent to Mob. Vet: Sec: Isola. fue	RS
ALBERT	11/10/16		Refill 1-20. Coy moved to area S.E. of ALBERT. Isola. fire.	RS

WAR DIARY or INTELLIGENCE SUMMARY

Army Form C. 2118

HEADQUARTERS COMPANY
4TH DIVISIONAL TRAIN

Place	Date	Hour	Summary of Events and Information	Remarks and references to Appendices
ALBERT	10/9/16		Refilling on road S. of ALBERT (ALBERT - BRAY-SUR-SOMME road) at 11.30 A.M. No. 74 Off. WHITE A.R.H. admitted to 140 F Field Amb. Ambulance. All troops happy returned to S.g. via mile sub. Q one	128
Do	11/9/16		Refilling as on 10/9. Rations received at 12 M. Troops issued to units Rather fine	129
Do	12/9/16		Refilling as on 10/9 on Somme Road as before. Rations received at 11.V.16 Blk Cattle etc. at Point of Rought. Fine Seasonable Weather. Strength	130
Do	15/9/16		Orders received to shift to Camp to Camp by 9 A.M. Troops working in 4 Camps. Replied at 11.30 A.M. All going short by 13 F 13th Inf. Over received tools just to the camp. Cart at Blab Rides at 7 p.m. rather fine. 2H.Q. with No. 137. Sent to Amble Vet Sec. for Arcandem & Grp. Rather fine	131
Do	16/9/16		Orders received to Re-camp to Cart at 1 am. Orgld. Refilling at 1.30 as before Rather fine. 74 6F 313 Off. WHITE. A.R.H. discharged 140 F Field Ambulance.	132

WAR DIARY
or
INTELLIGENCE SUMMARY

(Erase heading not required.)

Army Form C. 2118

Instructions regarding War Diaries and Intelligence Summaries are contained in F. S. Regs., Part II. and the Staff Manual respectively. Title Pages will be prepared in manuscript.

41st DIVISIONAL TRAIN

Place	Date	Hour	Summary of Events and Information	Remarks and references to Appendices
ALBERT	17/5/16		Refilling for supplies at MONTEBAN at 1 P.M. 1 Cycle Orderly to L.F. Army Ammle at QUERIEUX as runs regds. to to 3 Sullly KEETON. E.E. transferred to No 1 Base H.T. Depot HAVRE as supplies to establishment. Weather fine	[illeg.]
Do.	18/5/16		Refilling at same place as 1st inst. at 11 A.M. weather fine	[illeg.]
BUIRE	19/5/16		Company moved to BUIRE, arriving May 8.20 A.M. Refilled at BUIRE — @ R'PANCOURT casd at H.Q.R. Weather passing	[illeg.]
Do.	20/5/16		Refilling at 9 A.M. Some 898 to a 13th [illeg.] supplies given out returned to Camp. 1 Horse to Establish Cords., & bags further & H.Q. 9mg for Jas for 13 & BM.G., a 15 HHG. 2 S/S & sand Ships from Sich abroad. 1 H.G. Zire. 1 H. 9. Drum, 1 H. 9. Drum No 84 — attached to M.T. No.3 Coy Res	[illeg.]

1875 W: W593/826 1,000,000 4/15 J.B.C. & A. A.D.S.S./Forms/C. 2118.

WAR DIARY
or
INTELLIGENCE SUMMARY

(Erase heading not required.)

Army Form C. 2118

HEADQUARTERS COMPANY
41st DIVISIONAL TRAIN.

Place	Date	Hour	Summary of Events and Information	Remarks and references to Appendices
BUIRE	21/9/16		Refilling Same Spot as on 20th Inst: Guns heard at 2 P.M. Enemy Shelling in outskirts of BRAY. Units M.T.S. on wrecker. Weather Fine.	P.83
Do.	22/9/16		Refilling as on 20th Inst: 13 Supply lorry out returned to camp, firing Gun broken off refilling on 21st inst. 10th Q.O.R.W.K.R. English by M.V.S. No.2 from Cpl. Kirby Corpl. No. 2, 3 & 4 Coys. 9 R.B. Engaged by Shell fire at MONTAUBAN and two wounded. Weather Fine and bright.	P.83
Do.	23/9/16		Refilling 9 A.M. as at 22nd Inst: Lieut: Lett (Suire) & Camp of RECORD 4 P.M. arrived 5.45 P.M. 1 H.Q. Truck barnacled gun M.V.S. No.74 000576 Dr. BLOUNT. J. injured by being thrown from Lorry, admitted to hospital at Church St. Strength 24/9/16. Weather fine.	P.83
RECORD	24/9/16		Refilling 10 A.M. on road to RECORD Church. 1 H.Q. Lorry from cements: after on Strength. Weather Fine.	P.83

WAR DIARY or INTELLIGENCE SUMMARY

Army Form C. 2118

HEAD QUARTERS COMPANY
41st DIVISIONAL TRAIN

Place	Date	Hour	Summary of Events and Information	Remarks and references to Appendices
BECORDEL	25/5/16		Refilling 8-30 A.M. Same spot as on 24th. Issued fwd. All triggers wgn recalled from units.	RSS
Do.	26/5/16		Refilling 9 A.M. S. of O 25.E. 1 Orderly evacuated from M.V.S. & Buck St. Supply. Issued fwd.	RSS
Do.	27/5/16		Refilling as on 26th. All triggers & Supply wgn returned to units by Coy. Received 1 Orderly from Ammn Subs. Issued fwd. Ammn from ○	RSS
Do.	28/5/16		Refilling as usual. Supply wgn returned to units. Supply wgn drawn Rations Rations. No 74 105 (?) Sgt. Kings 12532 Sgt. Kings of H.Q. & 72066 Dr RUSSELL admitted 139 Field Ambulance. Issued fwd.	RSS
Do.	30/5/16		Routine as usual. Issued Ref. Officers Orderlies moved to new gd S.E. eng. the received ground in WHIT IN	RSS

Army Form C. 2118

WAR DIARY
or
INTELLIGENCE SUMMARY
(Erase heading not required.)

HEAD QUARTERS COMPANY.
41st DIVISIONAL TRAIN.

Instructions regarding War Diaries and Intelligence Summaries are contained in F. S. Regs., Part II. and the Staff Manual respectively. Title Pages will be prepared in manuscript.

Place	Date	Hour	Summary of Events and Information	Remarks and references to Appendices
OEEORDEL	30/5/16		Routine as usual. Weather fine.	Nil

M.B. Parker
HD.QRS. COY. 41st DIVL. TRAIN

1875 Wt. W 593/826 1,000,000 4/15 J.B.C. & A. A.D.S.S./Forms/C. 2118.

WAR DIARY or INTELLIGENCE SUMMARY

Army Form C. 2118

HEAD QUARTERS COMPANY
41st DIVISIONAL TRAIN

Place	Date	Hour	Summary of Events and Information	Remarks and references to Appendices
BECORDEL	1/10/16		Refilled at A.M. No 74 168310 Cpl. MIDDLEDITCH.A. discharged from 139 Fd Ambulance. reached base.	RB
Do.	2/10/16		Refitting at D H.Q. 2nd Lt. H.L. HOLLARD rejoined from base reached base	RB
Do.	3/10/16		Refitting at 12 P.H. 8 H.D. Lorry sent to M.V.S. & overhauled & stuck. Strength (4 Ehr.) reached base.	RB
Do.	4/10/16		Refilled 1 P.M. 2nd Lt: H.L. HOLLARD sent to Y Coy rejt station. 2nd Lt. Shore wounded by shrapnel & discharged. reached base.	RB
Do.	5/10/16		Refilling 10 A.M. No 74 0650□ Pte RUSSELL T. discharged from 138 Field Ambulance. reached base	RB
Do.	6/10/16		Refilled at A.M. No 74 Sgt. HINES.J. discharged for 365 Employ Coy. reached base	RB

Army Form C. 2118

HEAD QUARTERS COMPANY

DATE..........
No............
41st DIVISIONAL TRAIN

WAR DIARY
or
INTELLIGENCE SUMMARY
(Erase heading not required.)

Instructions regarding War Diaries and Intelligence Summaries are contained in F. S. Regs., Part II. and the Staff Manual respectively. Title Pages will be prepared in manuscript.

Place	Date	Hour	Summary of Events and Information	Remarks and references to Appendices
DECOUDEL	7/10/16		Supply Refilled at Méaulte (ALBERT) at 8 A.M. Refilled B.Ch. Leather fine.	[sig]
Do.	8/10/16		Refilled 1.500 P.M. Brother Ref Supply Column delivered at dump. Leather fine.	[sig]
Do.	9/10/16		Supply Refilled at Méaulte (ALBERT) at 12 P.M. refilled 9.45. Leather fine.	[sig]
Do.	10/10/16		Refilled 1.20 P.M. Supply Column delivered at dump. 1 H. Dr. Sergt. & Dr. V.S. Slaughter road in head & wearing 4 H.S. Turns for new small helm in Slaught. Leather fine.	[sig]
Do.	11/10/16		Refilling 1 P.M. Leather fine.	[sig]
Do.	12/10/16		Refilling 10-30 A.M. No T/3500 Dr. RUSSELL.T. sent to 138 R.F.A. units. Leather fine.	[sig]

… Army Form C. 2118

WAR DIARY
or
INTELLIGENCE SUMMARY

(Erase heading not required.)

HEAD QUARTERS COMPANY

41st DIVISIONAL TRAIN

Place	Date	Hour	Summary of Events and Information	Remarks and references to Appendices
ACCORDEL	13/10/16	9 A.M.	Captain R. H. King psd to Suth Midland (?) Casualty Clearing Station. Lt. C. TRIPP. psd. Engs. Trapuilly from No. 1 Fd Amb. Both sick.	RSL
Do.	14/10/16	5.15 P.M.	Weather fine.	RSL
Do.	15/10/16	6 P.M.	Weather fine.	RSL
Do.	16/10/16	9.30 A.M.	101999 Pte Wyatt attached to A/163 R.F.A. discharged to shell fire at FLERS. Weather showery.	RSL
Do.	17/10/16	12.30 P.M.	Weather fine.	RSL
Do.	18/10/16	3.45 P.M.	Showery	RSL
Do.	19/10/16	10.30 A.M.	No. 13755 Pr ELGER. T. admitted to y Cps(?) Casualty Station. Weather sick.	RSL
Do.	20/10/16	2.30 P.M.	Weather dull	RSL

WAR DIARY
or
INTELLIGENCE SUMMARY

(Erase heading not required.)

Army Form C. 2118

HEAD QUARTERS COMPANY

41st DIVISIONAL TRAIN.

Place	Date	Hour	Summary of Events and Information	Remarks and references to Appendices
RECORDE	21/10/16		Refile 1 P.M. No 72/352 Pr. DORRINGTON. E.A. 4TH/234 Pr. HAINE. F.T. admitted to 138 Field Ambulance. Further Enc.	RW
Do.	22/10/16		Refile 7.15 P.M. Leather Enc.	RW
Do.	23/10/16		Refile 12.30 P.M. Leather 18/C.	RW
Do.	24/10/16		Refile confield 20.A Army to leh Railway J Siseney. Syltified Supplies in Convoy, leaving camp at 3.30 A.M. Leather 18/C.	RW
Do.	25/10/16		Refile 1 P.M. Leather 18/C.	RW
Do.	26/10/16		Refile 4 P.M.) H.D. Lees. dischgd (Quilter.) No 72 Dr DORRINGTON. E.A. dischgd from 138 Field Ambulance. Leather Enc.	RW
Do.	27/10/16		Refile 5.30 P.M. No 73/026355 Dr ELISACK.T. dischgd from hospital. No 73/632033 Dr JOHNSON.A. Wacatta & shuck M. Stayes 20 hr inst (Km orby) Leather Gloves	RW

1875. Wt. W503/826 1,000,000 4/15 J.B.C. & A. A.D.S.S./Forms/C. 2118.

WAR DIARY
or
INTELLIGENCE SUMMARY

(Erase heading not required.)

Army Form C. 2118

HEAD QUARTERS COMPANY
41st DIVISIONAL TRAIN.

Place	Date	Hour	Summary of Events and Information	Remarks and references to Appendices
BECORDEL	28/10/16		Rifle 6 P.M. Weather fine	
Do	29/10/16		Rifle 5.30 P.M. 1 H.S. lamp exchanged; defective. 9 Pr Lt. A.L. HOLL A.R.D. Struck off Strength, to return above G.G. on regt. Occ. History Authority Q.M.G. A&Q No. 104.52/15 dated 17/10/16. 5 Guess Car Front Axles, Issued to H.Q. Coy, & 1st attached Co. No. 1 A. Coy.	
Do	30/10/16		Rifle 6 P.M. 1 H.S. lamp exchanged by Field Gun. Weather fine.	
Do	31/10/16		Leather Gun. Cartridge & Rifle etc. to be relieved up on firing fr. 1/11/16.	

H.D. Burke
Lt. Col.
HD. Qrs. Coy. 41st DIV.L TRAIN

March Orders by Lieut Colonel W. W. Molony A.S.C.

In continuation of Divisional Order, No 52. of 14th inst.

(1) **Order of March:-**

Passing Point Cross Roads RIBEMONT.
H. Qr Group to be clear by 8.30 am.
124th Infantry Bde Group to be clear by 9.10 am.
123rd " " " " " 9.50 am.
122nd " " " " " 10.30 am.

A.S.C. Brigade Coys (H.Qrs) will march with Brigade Groups. Supply Sections of Brigades (Horse Transport) will march empty with Divisional Train HQrs (D.H.Q. Group)

(2) **Billeting**

Representatives from each Group will report to O/C Column at QUERRIEU after arrival at QUERRIEU.
Each representative to be in possession of either horse or bicycle.

(3) **Rations.**

Refilling of Supplies for consumption on 17th inst will take place at ARGOEUVES on arrival of column.
Qr Mrs - representatives of units will join the Supply Section at QUERRIEU - march with same to Refilling Point. After Supplies have been delivered to Units Supply vehicles will rejoin Train HQrs (with D.H.Qr Group)

J. Brushcater
Captain a/a
41st Divisional Train

Issued at 12.30 pm.   Copies to :-
Camp Commandant.   10th Middlesex Regt
122nd I. Bde   Signal Coy R.E.
123rd "   Mobile Vety Section
124th "   Spare   2

WAR DIARY or INTELLIGENCE SUMMARY

Army Form C. 2118

(Erase heading not required.)

HEADQUARTERS COMPANY
41st DIVISIONAL TRAIN

Place	Date	Hour	Summary of Events and Information	Remarks and references to Appendices
BEORDEL	31/10/16		Refilled at R.H. by 1st Infanty half proceeding to MONTAUBAN. 2nd to BONNAY.	[sig]
BONNAY	1/11/16		Proceeded by march route to BONNAY leaving at 10 A.M & arriving 8 P.M. Refilled at BONNAY on arrival. Supply Vehicles travelling with Unit. 1 H.D. Mule died at BONNAY (Sick) No. T4/204 Dr: HAINE. F.T. Wounded & No. T4/5094 Dr: E.E. 36 C. No 24/10/16. (Attacks ceased 1.8h)	[sig]
Do.	2/11/16		Unit remained at BONNAY. Refilled at 9 A.M & second refill at 2 P.M. Supply wagons travelled with Unit filled 1st in Ovilleys line in Albert Wh: PRIOR D. & NOT 7604 Wh: GRATTA E rejoined the Coy from 4th Army Heavy Mobile Workshop.	[sig]

1875 Wt. W593/826 1,000,000 4/15 I.B.C. & A. A.D.S.S./Forms/C. 2118.

WAR DIARY
INTELLIGENCE SUMMARY

(Erase heading not required.)

Army Form C. 2118

HEADQUARTERS COMPANY
41st DIVISIONAL TRAIN.

Place	Date	Hour	Summary of Events and Information	Remarks and references to Appendices
VILLERS BOCAGE	3/11/16		Proceeded by march route from BOSQUAY to VILLERS BOCAGE. Starting 9 A.M., arriving 3-45 P.M. Rifle at VILLERS BOCAGE at 9 P.M. Weather fine.	
ORVILLE	4/11/16		Proceeded by march route to ORVILLE, leaving VILLERS BOCAGE at 9-30 A.M. & arriving 4-30 P.M. A.D. Force attached 1 Cook Sgt. H.Q. for Baggage & Supply Wgn) left at VILLERS BOCAGE suffering from debility. A.Q. despatched to 68 R.L.S. south Rifle at 6-30 A.M. on 5th. Weather fine.	
MONCHEL	6/11/16		Proceeded by march route to MONCHEL leaving ORVILLE 9 A.M. & arriving at 5-30 P.M. Rifle at BOUBERS-SUR-CANCHE at 7 P.M. NOTE Shoeing Sm: COPPING. G.E. admitted to BOUBERS Military Hospital. Weather fine.	

WAR DIARY or INTELLIGENCE SUMMARY

(Erase heading not required.)

Army Form C. 2118

HEAD QUARTERS COMPANY
DATE.................
NO..................
41st DIVISIONAL TRAIN.

Place	Date	Hour	Summary of Events and Information	Remarks and references to Appendices
ANVIN	6/1/16		Proceeded to Omer. Unit to ANVIN Starting at 6·30 A.M. & arriving 2·30 P.M. Refilled at 5·30 P.M. Weather fine. O.C. train visited Coy. on arrival at ANVIN.	RB
Do	7/1/16		Units remained at ANVIN. Refilled 3 P.M. S. No 2 Coy. Evacuated to base & struck off Strength. I.H.D. Wire No 46, attack Capt. R.A. KEMP. included in list on Area 623 29/10/16 recd: 2/11/16 to ENGLAND on 21/10/16 struck off Strgth. (Liason order 628 d. 30/10/16 & sec 3/11/16) Weather Very wet.	RB
Do	8/11/16		Unit remained at ANVIN. Refilled at 3 P.M. Weather Very wet.	RB
MOLINGHEM	9/11/16		Proceeded to MOLINGHEM Starting at 8·30 A.M. & arriving 3·30 P.M. Refilled 5·30 A.M. Weather fine. Billeted Royally, No 1 S.O.A.C. have left I.H.D. Lorry on line & much as left my my two officers & proceed.	RB
STAPLE	10/11/16		Proceeded to STAPLE Starting at 8·30 A.M. & arriving 1 P.M. Rifle B.P.N. Weather fine.	RB

WAR DIARY or INTELLIGENCE SUMMARY

Army Form C. 2118.

HEAD QUARTERS COMPANY
41st DIVISIONAL TRAIN.

Place	Date	Hour	Summary of Events and Information	Remarks and references to Appendices
RENINGHELST	11/11/16		Proceeded to march order to RENINGHELST. Starting 9:20 A.M. Arrived 6 P.M. No cattle. Bather fine. No 7's 8075 Shoeing Smith: COPPING G.C. died in No. 2 Casualty Clearing Station. Contr. G.H. COLGRAVE admitted into Stationary Hospital 65 M.T.; 151 Young Aux: H.Coy; on 8/11/16 & posted to 7th Eng; Vice Capt. I. KEMP.	
Do.	12/11/16		Supply wagons from Authead at WIPPENHOEK at 5:20 A.M. Dump of refills at 11 A.M. to H.Q. have occurred from scatter fire.	
Do.	15/11/16	10 A.M.	Supply wagons arrive from railhead at WIPPENHOEK at 7:30 A.M. Refilled T4 Driver ASH. W.R. T/36545 Dr. TARR. W. 122 520 admitted 190th Field Ambulance 56451 Dr. CLARKSON transferred from H.Q. 2nd Army 8/11/16 Weather fine.	

2449 Wt. W14957/M90 750,000 1/16 J.B.C. & A. Forms/C.2118/12.

Army Form C. 2118.

WAR DIARY
or
INTELLIGENCE SUMMARY
(Erase heading not required.)

HEAD QUARTERS COMPANY
DATE ....
No. ....
41st DIVISIONAL TRAIN.

Place	Date	Hour	Summary of Events and Information	Remarks and references to Appendices
RENINGHELST	14/11/16		Supply wagons drew from WIPPENHOEK at 10 a.m. Nine H.D. horses sent to Mobile Veterinary Section for evacuation and were struck off the strength. Weather fine.	JR
"	15/11/16		Reached refilling as on 14/11/16. One H.D. horse died and was struck off the strength. T4/122820 Dr. ASH W.R. to camps from 140th Field Ambulance. Weather fine.	JR
"	16/11/16		Reached refilling as on 15/11/16. Baggage wagons to & from units. Weather fine.	JR
"	17/11/16		Reached & refilling as on 16/11/16. T3/037,533 Dr. JOHNSON H. rejoined for duty on 15/11/16 and taken on the strength. T/365/77 Dr. WALKER R.J. to 140th Field Ambulance. Weather fine.	JR
"	18/11/16		Reached refilling as on 17/11/16. T/30844 Dr. SHORTER F. admitted 140th Field Ambulance. Weather wet.	JR

Army Form C. 2118.

WAR DIARY
or
INTELLIGENCE SUMMARY

(Erase heading not required.)

HEAD QUARTERS COMPANY
DATE..........
No. ....
41st DIVISIONAL TRAIN.

Instructions regarding War Diaries and Intelligence Summaries are contained in F. S. Regs., Part II. and the Staff Manual respectively. Title Pages will be prepared in manuscript.

Place	Date	Hour	Summary of Events and Information	Remarks and references to Appendices
H.Q. RENINGHELST	19/11/16		Reissue & refilling as on 18/11/16. T/36332 Dr SELWOOD W.J. admitted to C.C.S. T/094200 Dr CARLANE J. discharged from 140th Field Ambulance. Weather wet.	P
do	20/11/16		Reissue & refilling as on 19/11/16. T/36545 Dr FARR W. T/36577 Dr WALKER J. and Dr CARLANE J. discharged from 140th Field Ambulance. One H.D. horse left at VILLERS BOCAGE on 4/11/16 struck off the strength. Ret. Train order 707 dated 20.11.16. Weather fine.	P
do	21/11/16		Supply wagons refilled direct from railhead WIPPENHOEK at 7.30. Weather fine.	P
do:	22/11/16		Refilling as on 21st inst. Weather fine.	P

2449 Wt. W14957/M90 750,000 1/16 J.B.C. & A. Forms/C.2118/12.

Army Form C. 2118.

WAR DIARY
or
INTELLIGENCE SUMMARY
(Erase heading not required.)

HEAD QUARTERS COMPANY
DATE.............
No..............
41st DIVISIONAL TRAIN.

Instructions regarding War Diaries and Intelligence Summaries are contained in F. S. Regs., Part II. and the Staff Manual respectively. Title Pages will be prepared in manuscript.

Place	Date	Hour	Summary of Events and Information	Remarks and references to Appendices
RENINGHELST	23/1/16		Rejoining on duty WR. No: TS/3607 W. Cpl. RICHARDS.E. Admitted 140 Field Ambulance. No: T/30844 Dr: SAORTER.F.T. discharged 140 Field Ambulance. No: T/13572 Dr: GORTON.C. admitted 140 Field Ambulance. Sick — one.	[sgd]
Do	24/1/16		Rejoining at 222nd & Army Over Transferred to No: 2 Coy. No:T4/057193 Dr: HARPER.T. No:T4/232193 Dr: SAAW.F. No:T4/034007 Dr: TAYLOR.A. & No:T4/235961 Dr: NILSON J.E. sick — one.	[sgd]
Do	25/1/16		Rejoining at a 20 Div. 1 O.R. de-linked No:T/022082 a/SSgt: BULL.W. transferred to No: 3 Coy. No:T/18519 a/Sgt: VOSPER.G.S. from No: 2 Coy. Sick 1st R.	[sgd]

WAR DIARY
INTELLIGENCE SUMMARY
(Erase heading not required.)

Army Form C. 2118.

HEADQUARTERS COMPANY
DATE..................
No. ....
41st DIVISIONAL TRAIN.

Place	Date	Hour	Summary of Events and Information	Remarks and references to Appendices
RENINGHELST.	26/11/16		Routine as usual. 2nd Lt: PAGE. E. joined from 10th Reserve Park. No 74/457 a/Sgt. CHURCHILL. W.A.M. reverted to permanent grade of driver & G.C.M. & transferred to No: 4 Coy. Breakfast one.	RnB
Do:	27/11/16		Routine as usual. Breakfast one.	RnB
Do:	28/11/16		Routine as usual. Nos.TS/607 1st Cpl. RICHARDS. C. discharged from two R.A. No TS/76446 a/Cpl. MEADOWS. E. admitted 143 FA. No T4/057948 Dr. BOWMAN R. discharged 12th C.C.S. Breakfast one.	RnB
Do:	29/11/16		Routine as usual. Breakfast one. Mule Depot (HT-43) No T4/240534 Dr. HIGSON. L.J.	RnB
Do	30/11/16		Routine as usual. Breakfast one.	RnB

R. Bradley
O.C. Hd. Qrs. Coy. 41st Divl. Train

WAR DIARY or INTELLIGENCE SUMMARY

Army Form C. 2118.

HEAD QUARTERS COMPANY
41st DIVISIONAL TRAIN.

Place	Date	Hour	Summary of Events and Information	Remarks and references to Appendices
RENINGHELST	1/12/16		Parade at 7.30 A.M. No.1/13472 Dr. GORTON. E. discharged 2nd Canadian C.C.S. Beacon line.	
Do.	2/12/16		Parade at 7.30 A.M., 1 riding horse transferred to 59th M.V.S. Supply to 53rd (Highland) No. T3/369 S/Sgt. FRANKS. J. admitted to 140 Field Amb. The following Other Ranks 15th Reft. for duty:	
			No: 54772 S/Sgt SATTERTHWAITE. W. to No.2 Coy	
			" 2870 Sgt. JENKINS. W. " 3 "	
			" 0444.03 L/Cpl. ASHWORTH. J. " 3 "	
			" 0724.19 Pte TEMPLE. E.H. " 4 "	
			" 54192 Pte. CARTLEDGE. E.A.S. " 4 "	
			" 860192	
			" 54129	
			" 072 29	
			PTE. RUBIN from No.2 Coy.	
			" McKAY " 2 "	
			L/Cpl ROSSER " 3 "	
			S/Sgt BARKER. G.A. " 4 "	
			Pte. WHYTE. J. " 4 "	Isaka Line

WAR DIARY
or
INTELLIGENCE SUMMARY

(Erase heading not required.)

Army Form C. 2118.

HEAD QUARTERS COMPANY
DATE...........
No............
41st DIVISIONAL TRAIN.

Place	Date	Hour	Summary of Events and Information	Remarks and references to Appendices
RENINGHELST	3/2/16		Rcpld D.P.H. Chan Lilly No. T/36546 Dr: FARR.W. admitted No 15 Field Amb: T/24836 Dr: BARRETT. F. admitted No 15 Field Amb: Received 6 H.Q. Coys Demands. 2 H.D. Luke Star E. S.D. W. In. V.S. & Shuck Weather fine.	J.B.S.
Do	4/2/16		Rcpld at 7.30 A.M. No T/2SR A5886/16 Rector Infected by D.E. Iran at 2.15 P.M. On Weather fine. Sergeant at an aerodrome.	J.B.S.
Do	5/2/16		Rcpld 7.30 A.M. No. T/2SR A/CS.M. WELFORD awarded 15 Demonstration Grade 1906 Weather Snowing.	J.B.S.
Do	6/2/16		Rcpld 7.30 A.M. No: T/84417 Sgt. BEACH. J. admitted No 15 Field Amb: No T/ Ranger Dr: SAILES transferred from Divn H.T. Depot. 240046 Weather fine.	J.B.S.

WAR DIARY
or
INTELLIGENCE SUMMARY

(Erase heading not required.)

Army Form C. 2118.

Place	Date	Hour	Summary of Events and Information	Remarks and references to Appendices
RENINGHELST.	5/10/16		Rifle 10 A.M. No. T/9 Dr. BARRETT. F. struck W. Shayk (During R.A. admitted to No.5 R.A. & wounded) No. T/S 7486 Sddlr. Cpl. USHER. J. admitted 140 F.A. No. T/SR 7906 Sgt: WELFORD. A.J. transferred to No. 3 Coy. & No. T/6 Sgt: PHILLIPS. A Jnr No. 3 Coy: Traktor Sturing	(Sgd)
Do.	8/10/16		Rifle 7.20 A.M. Traktor Sturing.	Sd. (Sgd)
Do.	9/10/16		Rifle 7.20 A.M. No. T/5945 Dr. TARR. W. discharged 140 F.A. Conv: No. T/05580 Traktor Stury & Shun.	(Sgd)
Do.	10/10/16		Rifle 7.30 A.M. No. T/36681 Dr. COLES. T.G. admitted 140 F.A. No. T/05580 Dr. FRANKS. J. discharged 140 F.A. Traktor W.C.	(Sgd)
Do.	11/10/16		Rifle 7.30 A.M. O.C. Train inspected transport section & eng: traktor.	(Sgd)

WAR DIARY or INTELLIGENCE SUMMARY

Army Form C. 2118

HEAD QUARTERS COMPANY
41st DIVISIONAL TRAIN

Place	Date	Hour	Summary of Events and Information	Remarks and references to Appendices
RENINGHELST	12/10/16	Refille 7.20 A.M.	No. T/2407 Sergt. BEACH. J. discharged 140⁰ R.F.A. No. T4 050 Dr. KAY. W. admitted 140⁰ F.A. Butcher Group.	R&B
Do.	13/10/16	Refille 7.20 A.M.	Butcher I/C.	R&B
Do.	14/10/16	Refille 7.20 A.M.	Proceeded 1st line transport of sixteen A.S.C. all ranks. Chief: G.H. COLEGRAVE transferred to No. 4 Coy; Lt: E. TRIPP from No. 2 Coy; 2/Lt: H.N. PAGE to No 2 Coy. No T/4621 Dr: VINCENT. J to No. 4 Coy & No.T3/096673 Dr: PEARCE A. J BEEVERS F from No. 4 Coy. No.T4/094010 admitted 140⁰ F.A. Butcher Gme.	R&B
Do.	15/10/16	Refille 7.20 A.M.	Butcher Gme.	R&B
Do.	16/10/16	Refille 7.20 A.M.	No. S4/040,679 Pte: BOSOMWORTH. E. admitted 138⁰ F.A. Butcher Gme.	R&B

Army Form C. 2118

WAR DIARY
or
INTELLIGENCE SUMMARY
(Erase heading not required.)

HEADQUARTERS COMPANY
DATE...........
No..............
41st DIVISIONAL TRAIN

Instructions regarding War Diaries and Intelligence Summaries are contained in F.S. Regs., Part II. and the Staff Manual respectively. Title Pages will be prepared in manuscript.

Place	Date	Hour	Summary of Events and Information	Remarks and references to Appendices
REMINGHELST	17/10/16		Refile 7-30 A.M. Weather fine. Officers Quarters moved from Jann Ruge & hut by higher ground.	RSS
Do	18/10/16		Refile 7-30 A.M. No 74050 Pr. RAY W. discharged 898 Northumbrian C.C.S. No 15409 Pr. Turner ROBERTS G. Sick list. Sent hospital to Eng. No: 34670 Pte BOSOMWORTH E discharged 173rd Field Am; Weather fine.	RSS
Do	19/10/16		Refile 7-30 A.M. Weather fine.	RSS
Do	20/10/16		Refile 10-30 A.M. Clock changed to 10-30 a.m. the Dowels) Weather fine.	RSS
Do	21/10/16		Refile 10-30 A.M. No: 75/59 Sadd: Gr. USHER J. discharged 140 R.F.A. No: 74530 Sgt. MULCAHY E.F. admitted 138 F.A. Weather BC.	RSS
Do	22/10/16		Refile 10-30 A.M. Weather BC.	RSS

WAR DIARY
or
INTELLIGENCE SUMMARY

(Erase heading not required.)

Army Form C. 2118

HEAD QUARTERS COMPANY
41st DIVISIONAL TRAIN.

Place	Date	Hour	Summary of Events and Information	Remarks and references to Appendices
RENINGHELST.	23/10/16		Vehicle 10.30 A.M. No. T3/8863 Dr. KELLY. J.J. admitted 40.F.A. Brother Sherry.	Pes
Do.	24/10/16		Vehicle 9.30 A.M. No. T4/044653 Sgt. McLEAHY. C.F. discharged 188 F.A. Brother Gue.	Pes
Do.	25/10/16		Vehicle 12.30 P.M. (Main lake) Brother Shearer.	Pes
Do.	26/10/16		Vehicle 10.30 A.M. T4/9 Pte Ret E.505 N.Y.S. 9 8 truck M.035 Brother Gue.	Pes
Do.	27/10/16		Vehicle 10.30 A.M. Brother Gue.	Pes
Do.	28/10/16		Vehicle 10.30 A.M. No. T2/8863 Dr. KELLY. J.J. discharged No. 7. A brother Gue.	Pes

Army Form C. 2118

HEAD QUARTERS COMPANY

DATE ....
No. ....

41st DIVISIONAL TRAIN.

WAR DIARY
or
INTELLIGENCE SUMMARY
(Erase heading not required.)

Instructions regarding War Diaries and Intelligence Summaries are contained in F.S. Regs, Part II. and the Staff Manual respectively. Title Pages will be prepared in manuscript.

Place	Date	Hour	Summary of Events and Information	Remarks and references to Appendices
RENINGHELST.	29/10/16		Reveille 10.30 A.M. No. 74180 Dr. CARLANE. J. admitted No F.A. S.H.D. & 1 Ounce Struck off Strength. 1 A.D. 91 Ounce posted to Eng. from Remounts. Brother Nursing.	RSs
Do.	30/10/16		Reveille 10 Ambulance. No. CT3 099 446 Cpl. MEADOWS. C. joined Coy. from Base Depot (H.T. 28). Captain PolFARD URQUHART joined Coy. from 30th Div. Train Att. Brother Nursing	RS
Do.	31/10/16		Reveille 10.20 A.M. Brother Evac. Inds.	RS

B.D. Parker Captain.

WAR DIARY or INTELLIGENCE SUMMARY

Army Form C. 2118

HEAD QUARTERS COMPANY
41st DIVISIONAL TRAIN.

Place	Date	Hour	Summary of Events and Information	Remarks and references to Appendices
RENINGHELST	1/1/17		Refile 12 Noon. 74B. Coys. discharged. Weather fine.	
Do	2/1/17		Refile 10.20 A.M. Weather fine.	
Do	3/1/17		Refile 10.20 A.M. Weather fine.	
Do	4/1/17		Refile 10.20 A.M. No T4/1000 Dr. CARLANE. J. discharged for. 140 Field Am. Weather showery	
Do	5/1/17		Refile 10.20 A.M. No T4/030 Dr. MOORE. A.S. & No. T3/4446 Cpl. MEADOWS. C. admitted 140 F.A. Weather fine.	
Do	8/1/17		Refile 1.45 p.m. No T4/065964 Dr. WAITE. E.A. & No. 108/315 Cpl. WHITE. A.H. admitted 140 F.A. Weather showery	
Do	9/1/17		Refile 10.20 A.M. No. T4/010 Dr. PEARCE. A.J. evacuated from 140 C.C.S. Weather fine. On 19/1/16 & struck off strength.	

WAR DIARY
or
INTELLIGENCE SUMMARY

(Erase heading not required.)

Army Form C. 2118

Place	Date	Hour	Summary of Events and Information	Remarks and references to Appendices
RENINGHELST	8/11/17	Reveille 10.30 A.M.	No. 78/158313 Cpl. WAITE. A. R.A. No. 78/158488 Sgdl. Cpl. USHER. J. admitted 140 F.A. No. 74/158313 Cpl. WAITE. A. R.A. discharged 140 F.A. Strike fine	R.B.
Do.	9/11/7	Reveille 10.30 A.M.	4.H.D. Luna & 1 other received gun wounds slinney.	R.B.
Do.	10/11/7	Reveille 11.10 A.M.	2 Infy. Simo & drinks sent to 4/1st Div: Training School at STEENVOORDE. No. 74/25031 Pr. COLES. F.G. discharged 140 F.A. Fine.	R.B.
Do.	11/11/7	Reveille 12.30 P.M.	No. 74/254922 Pr. CROCKER. E. admitted 128 F.A. No. A30 Pr. MOORE. A-S & No. 74/059654 Pr. WAITE. E.A. Wounded to C.C.S. & struck off strength.	R.B.
Do.	12/11/7	Reveille 11.15 A.M.	Strike slinney.	R.B.
Do.	13/11/7	Reveille 11.30 A.M.	Strike very bad.	R.B.

WAR DIARY
or
INTELLIGENCE SUMMARY

(Erase heading not required.)

Army Form C. 2118

HEAD QUARTERS COMPANY
41st DIVISIONAL TRAIN

Place	Date	Hour	Summary of Events and Information	Remarks and references to Appendices
RENINGHELST	14/1/17		H.Q. took over + struck WG 15/1/17. Isolation gone.	
Do	15/1/17	Reple 10.30 A.M.		
		Reple 10. A.M.	No: 74950 Pr. WATSON. W. No: T/4615 Dr. McLAUGHLIN. M. & No: T/383 Dr. ASHWIN. J. from line depot posted to Eng. T/4 Dr. BOWMAN 05/7009 R. admitted 130 field Amb. Isolation gone.	Regd
Do	16/1/17	Reple 10. A.M.	No: T/4510 S.S.M. YORK E.H. No: T/3540 S.S.M. DUGGAN. H.J. transferred to Eng. from 140.5. F.A. Gone sick.	Regd
Do	17/1/17	Reple 10. A.M.	No: T/4383 Dr. Harris ROBERTS. E. transferred to Rate depot from 140.5. F.A. Gone sick.	Regd
		No: T/7005 Dr. SMART. J.W. 6 134 F.A. Gone sick.		
Do	18/1/17	Reple 10. A.M.	No: T/4000 Dr. CROCKER. E Evacuated to C.C.S. from 05/4000 Dr. SHEA Jr. Isolation lost.	Regd
		Church at Sheep R.		

WAR DIARY
or
INTELLIGENCE SUMMARY

Army Form C. 2118

HEAD QUARTERS COMPANY
41st DIVISIONAL TRAIN

Place	Date	Hour	Summary of Events and Information	Remarks and references to Appendices
RENINGHELST	19/11/17		Refill 10 A.M. Nos. T.V. 1146 Col. M.E.D O/i/C. & No. T.S. 5/186 S/Lt. Ch. Usher R.N. Evacuated to C.C.S. 2 O/R or Shght. Isenberger. One	RM
Do	20/11/17		Horse Cable changed to 7 A.M. From this, refilled 10 A.M. Isenberger. One 2 Shgs.	RM
Do	21/11/17		Little Late 10.30 A.M. Rather fine. Serke POW	RM
Do	22/11/17		Refill 7 A.M. J.H.D. Coyle Dispatched. 12 G.S. wagons 24 horses (49) under 2 Lt. Boyden 10 Coyden, 1 Sergt. Sent to DHQ Ypres R.G.A. to accompany School unit during training. Weather fine 9 Frost.	RM
Do	23/11/17		Refill 7 A.M. No T.W. 06/2053 2.Lt CULPIN R.N. admitted 138 F.A. Weather fine 9 Frost.	RM
Do	24/11/17		Refill 2 P.M. T.H.D. Lorus sent E.N.V.S. No T.W. 012/045 2. Lt BOWMAN. R. 138 F.A. discharged 138 F.A. Weather fine. Frosty.	RM
Do	25/11/17		Refill 10.30 A.M. No T.W. 5/22100 2.Lt CULPIN R. discharged 138 F.A. 5/22100 2.Lt CULPIN R. And Frost	RM

WAR DIARY
or
INTELLIGENCE SUMMARY

Army Form C. 2118

Place	Date	Hour	Summary of Events and Information	Remarks and references to Appendices
REMINGHELST	26/11/17	Refile 1-25 P.M. No. T4900 Dr. SMART J.W. Evacuated to C.C.S. 2/4th Inf. & Strength. Rank Sgt.		Ref
Do.	27/11/17	Refile 3-45 P.M. No. T4900 Dr. CROCKER.E. rejoined from C.C.S. 60/T4900 Dr. RILEY P.S. transferred from 557/476 C.S.M. withdrawn the Strength. No. 2 Coy. Rank Sgt.		Ref
Do.	28/11/17	Refile 1-20 P.M. No. T4917 Dr. Smith. JONES.H. transferred from Base Depot. 65% T3967 Strength Rank Sgt.		Ref
Do.	29/11/17	Refile 10 A.M. No. T515 Dr. McLOUGHLIN.M. & 16795 Dr. WILSHER.J. wounded 166 F.S.A. 574/ST Rank Sgt.		Ref
Do.	30/11/17	Refile 2 P.M. H. Large steel to struck W. Baugh R. Rank Sgt. Slight Brns.		Ref
Do.	31/11/17	Refile 7 A.M. Rank Susp. Slight Brns.		Ref

WAR DIARY
or
INTELLIGENCE SUMMARY
(Erase heading not required.)

Army Form C. 2118

HEAD QUARTERS COMPANY
41st DIVISIONAL TRAIN.

Place	Date	Hour	Summary of Events and Information	Remarks and references to Appendices
RENINGHELST	1/2/17		Refile 7 A.M. Water fine - Frost.	Pope
Do.	2/2/17	7 A.M.	Refile 7 A.M. No.1 S/Sgt. BEACH. J. & No.73 Pte. HALLETT.P. admitted 188 Field Ambulance. Water fine Frost.	Pope
Do.	3/2/17	12 Noon	Refile 12 Noon. No.54 S/Sgt 256 Pte. WILSHER. E. Wounded to C.C.S. On 30/1/17. Water Sh. Water fine Frost.	Pope
Do.	4/2/17	12 Noon	Refile 12 Noon. Water Frost.	Pope
Do.	5/2/17	1 P.M.	Refile 1 P.M. Water Frost.	Pope
Do.	6/2/17	8.30 A.M.	Refile 8.30 A.M. Water Frost.	Pope
Do.	7/2/17	10.30 A.M.	Refile 10.30 A.M. No.7 Dvr. McLOUGHLIN. M. Wounded to No.15.15 Dr. 31/5/15 C.C.S. & Struck off. Water Frost.	Pope

WAR DIARY
or
INTELLIGENCE SUMMARY

(Erase heading not required.)

Army Form C. 2118

Instructions regarding War Diaries and Intelligence Summaries are contained in F.S. Regs., Part II. and the Staff Manual respectively. Title Pages will be prepared in manuscript.

HEADQUARTERS COMPANY
41st DIVISIONAL TRAIN

Place	Date	Hour	Summary of Events and Information	Remarks and references to Appendices
RENINGHELST	8/2/17	11.30 A.M.	Refile. Weather frosty.	
Do.	9/2/17	1.30 P.M.	Refile. Posted to Estb: No T/24017 Sergt. BEACH. S. 10 A.D. have received for Remunds to Hote 121 O.Q. Dr. HALLET. P. Wounded. 15 E.C.S. Struck off. Frosty.	
Do.	10/2/17	2.45 P.M.	Refile. Weather frosty.	
Do.	11/2/17	12.15 P.M.	Refile. Weather frosty.	
Do.	12/2/17	10 A.M.	Refile. Weather fine. Thaws.	
Do.	13/2/17	10.30 A.M.	Refile. Supply & Trigger ingots Shirt to 187/Bde R.F.A. Weather finer of night B.B.G.	
Do.	14/2/17	8.30 A.M.	Refile. L.B. A.S. BLACK sent to Canadian C.C.S. slight wound knee. Joint. Thawy from sun like. Pr.B.C.	

WAR DIARY
or
INTELLIGENCE SUMMARY

Army Form C. 2118

HEADQUARTERS COMPANY
41st DIVISIONAL TRAIN.

Place	Date	Hour	Summary of Events and Information	Remarks and references to Appendices
REMINGHELST	15/2/17	8.30 A.M.	Refile. Sgt. BEACH J. reported for C.C.S. & later to Slaughter. No 54 D4017 Sgt. BARKER G.A. admitted 140 F.A. Fine. Cplus.	[sig]
Do.	16/2/17	10. A.M.	Refile. Weather fine.	[sig]
Do.	17/2/17	7.30 A.M.	Refile. No. T3575 Pte. LOUGHLIN M. reported from C.C.S. & later to Slaughter. Weather fine.	[sig]
Do.	18/2/17	7.45 A.M.	Refile. No. 54 D4017 Sgt. BARKER G.A. discharged from 140 F.A. Weather fine.	[sig]
Do.	19/2/17	11 A.M.	Refile. No T3575 Pte. ELBECK T. admitted 1835 F.A. 1. H.Q. Sub. wounded S.M.S. & Stuck H.C. Fine & Sub. in Q.S. 48.5.	[sig]
Do.	20/2/17		Refile Hour changed to 5.45 A.M. Actually refilled ak 10.30 A.M. Sr. SCOTT J.S.S. Rgn S.1) for A.D. Lines reported hrs from Divisional Training School. L.S.C.	[sig]

Army Form C. 2118

WAR DIARY
or
INTELLIGENCE SUMMARY

(Erase heading not required.)

Instructions regarding War Diaries and Intelligence Summaries are contained in F. S. Regs., Part II. and the Staff Manual respectively. Title Pages will be prepared in manuscript.

Place	Date	Hour	Summary of Events and Information	Remarks and references to Appendices
RENINGHELST	21/2/17	10.50 A.M.	Baken one.	
Do.	22/2/17	10.25 A.M.	People No. 74/8/17 Dr THORPE, A. admitted to 1/3rd F.A. suffering from self inflicted wound through right side, lung changed, gathering wild. Ring cleaned. Baker one.	
Do.	23/2/17	10 A.M.	Baker one.	
Do.	24/2/17	9.20 A.M.	No.75 Pte/a S.S. Dickenson, J.G. reacted to Remount Depot of Saddler driver at our request. Baker one.	
Do.	25/2/17	9.30 A.M.	Baker one.	
Do.	26/2/17	9.40 A.M.	No.76 Driver 16 G 8 W/n & 32 H.S. Rogers Lengted Nrn 13 189 1856 R.F.A. Rds. to 2 nd line transport of 9th Army field Artillery Brigade. Name of driver given on our request. Baker one.	
Continued on Rear Sheet				

WAR DIARY
or
INTELLIGENCE SUMMARY

(Erase heading not required.)

Army Form C. 2118

HEAD QUARTERS COMPANY
41st DIVISIONAL TRAIN.

Place	Date	Hour	Summary of Events and Information	Remarks and references to Appendices
RENINGHELST.			Dr. JONES. B. T4/515 Dr. TURVEY. T. T4/515 KING. J.H. T4/514	
Enlisted from Base	22/12/17		" BARRATT. G.I. T3/032 " POWELL. J.J. T1/58 SCOTT. J. T/88238	
"			" NUNN. J.H. T4/0 " DAVIES. R.J. T4/635 WOOD. J. T4/545	
"			" CARLANE. J T4/9001 " CAMDEN. G. T4/227 WALKER. J. T3/677	
"			" BRADLEY. A T4/305 " DURRANT. W. T4/512 WALLACE. T. T/257	
			" RUSSELL. T. T/63066	(RSB)
			1 H.D. have died. Lt. A.S. BLACK returned to duty from Canadian G.C.S.	
			State fine.	
Do.	27/12/17		Refile 8.20 A.M. 1 Subaltern, 1 Sergeant, 91 Bngrs. began Enfield Short Rotary	(RSB)
			130 Rgs R.R.A. Weather fine.	
Do.	28/12/17		Refile 8.35 A.M. Weather fine.	(RSB)

B. Banks Major
O.C. HD. QRS. COY. 41st DIVL. TRAIN.

Army Form C. 2118

HEAD QUARTERS COMPANY
DATE............
No................
41st DIVISIONAL TRAIN

WAR DIARY
or
INTELLIGENCE SUMMARY
(Erase heading not required.)

Instructions regarding War Diaries and Intelligence Summaries are contained in F.S. Regs., Part II. and the Staff Manual respectively. Title Pages will be prepared in manuscript.

Place	Date	Hour	Summary of Events and Information	Remarks and references to Appendices
QENINGHELST	1/3/17	Reveille 6.45 AM.	The following Strength Ror Places:— from H.Q. Coy 16: Crain W.D.S. SH/6126 S/Sgt. TAYLOR W.P. 70/4113 Sgt. TAIT J.J. Dr. BALDWIN P.J. S6/6126 M/2/116 T/4/6167 044113 Cpl. EARDLEY W. S/4/465 Cpl. ROSSER J.O. 022/67 Dr. DAVISON R.G. M/2/116 03/3316 080/465 T/3/82 T/1748 Dr. DUGGAN J. M/2/3341 Cpl. GOWER A.V. T/4/413 Dr. WITHERS A.S. 0/1748 Dr. OXLEY J. 133351 240/413 24/78 Coy No: 3 Bdg. T/S Dr. Saddler DICKENSON J.G. from No: 3 Coy to H.Q. Coy 5061 Saddler Cpl. CARROLL R.J.S. Coy No: 4 Bdg: No T/5 T/5/8 Brothers in. Law YOSPER G.S.	[signature]
Do:	2/3/17	Reveille 6.45 A.M.	2 H.O. Drivers Wounded to 59th M.V.S. struck off Strength Brothers in Law	[signature]
Do:	3/3/17	Reveille 10 A.M.	Brothers in Law J.S.L.	[signature]

WAR DIARY
or
INTELLIGENCE SUMMARY
(Erase heading not required.)

Army Form C. 2118

HEADQUARTERS COMPANY

Place	Date	Hour	Summary of Events and Information	Remarks and references to Appendices
RENINGHELST.	4/3/17	Rflle 9.45 A.M.	The undermentioned details proceeded to A.H.T. Dept at ABBEVILLE to Osed. Lt. E. TRIPP i/c [Employ's Own Van Platts ground.] No.7232 Dr. ASHWIN. J. No.7230 Dr. BARTLETT. H. J. No.7234 Dr. JONES. JA. No.7235 Dr. THOMPSON. J. No.74252 Dr. WATSON. W. 10. H.D. Lorries. E.G.S. Wgn. Omk 10" & 16 S.G. P.D.E. S.Q. Lorries. Brake Fine.	RB
Do.	5/3/17	Rflle 9.50 A.M.	Rgbr Gul J. sucs. H.Q. Lrun Wheener fried arc	RB
Do.	6/3/17	Rflle 9.50 A.M.	Brake Fine.	RB
Do.	7/3/17	Rflle 9.45 A.M.	54473 Sgt. BARKER. G.A. 1s No.3 coy; No 54/492 pt: Sgt: JENKINS. W.D. 2nd No. 3 coy; 15 RR. Bde; & No.844044 Brake dry & Very windy	RB
Do.	8/3/17	Rflle 10.45 A.M.	Dr. ELBECK. T. No.73/255 Dr. ELBECK. T. discharged 128 F.A. She Snow, very windy	RB

WAR DIARY
or
INTELLIGENCE SUMMARY

(Erase heading not required.)

Army Form C. 2118

HEADQUARTERS COMPANY

Place	Date	Hour	Summary of Events and Information	Remarks and references to Appendices
RENINGHELST	8/3/17	Rifle 9-50 A.M.	Slight fall of snow.	[sig]
Do	10/3/17	Rifle 9-45 A.M.	Weather fine & frosty	[sig]
Do	11/3/17	Rifle 9-40 A.M. 186 B.F.A.	No. 74029 Dr. PARRETT. G.E. admitted to 51 Stationery amb.	[sig]
Do	12/3/17	Rifle 9-30 A.M.	Weather showery	[sig]
Do	13/3/17	Rifle 9-30 A.M. A & B Batteries 187	J.H.D. battery died Church St. Offr. wagon & Horse kill'd. Thy mul. Weather fine	[sig]
Do	14/3/17	Rifle 9-40 A.M.	Weather fine	[sig]
Do	15/3/17	Rifle 9-45 A.M.	Weather fine	[sig]
Do	16/3/17	Rifle 9-45 A.M.	Weather fine all waggons of Headquarters, C & D Batteries 187 Brigade returned to camp. 1 waggon returned from STEENWORD	W.B.F.?

WAR DIARY
or
INTELLIGENCE SUMMARY

Army Form C. 2118

HEADQUARTERS COMPANY
41st DIVISIONAL TRAIN

Place	Date	Hour	Summary of Events and Information	Remarks and references to Appendices
Remington	17/7		Refill 9.50 A.M. No T4/094029 Dr PARRATT.T.C. evacuated to C.C.S. on 17th inst. struck off the strength. Weather fine.	M.B.P.M
do	18/7		Refill 9. HEATH. No T4/042-383 Dr. and GILDART.N. admitted to 138 Field Ambulance. Weather fine. Captain B.W. PARKER proceeded on leave to ENGLAND.	M.B.P.M
do	19/7		Refill 9.30 A.M. Weather fine. Headquarters Det. & Company Parts.	M.B.P.M
do	20/7		Refill 7.30 A.M. Weather fine. Refilled before instead of after 6th DIVISION	M.B.P.M
do	21/7		Refill 7.30 A.M. Weather fine.	M.B.P.M
do	22/7		Refill 9.30 A.M. No T4/SR/02978 Driver OXLEY.N. transferred from Headquarters 41st Div. Train. No T3/027033 Dr JOHNSON.H. transferred to Headquarters 41st Div. Train. Snow fell at intervals	M.B.P.M
do	23/7		Refill 7.30 A.M. Weather fine.	M.B.P.M
do	24/7		Refill 7.30 A.M. Official time advanced 1 hour at 11 p.m. Weather fine	M.B.P.M
do	25/7		Refill 9 A.M. Weather fine	M.B.P.M
do	26/7		Refill 2 p.m. Weather wet	M.B.P.M

WAR DIARY or INTELLIGENCE SUMMARY

(Erase heading not required.)

Army Form C. 2118

HEAD QUARTERS COMPANY
41st DIVISIONAL TRAIN.

Place	Date	Hour	Summary of Events and Information	Remarks and references to Appendices
Tournai/Adet	27/3/17		Refill 1.30 p.m. Two H.D. horses admitted to 52nd M.V.S. Weather fine	M.B.P.M
do	28/3/17		Refill 2 p.m. No T4/042363 Dr GILBART J. discharged from 138 Field Ambulance. No T4/194738 Dr SADLER KIBBLE W.W. transferred from Base Depot (H.T.+S.) and Taken on strength. Weather fine. CAPTAIN V.H. PENNELL rejoined from leave.	M.B.P.M
do	29/3/17		Refill 10. A.M. Weather showery. No T2/018184 Dr WILSON. R.R. and Capt PENNELL V.H. admitted to 138 Field ambulance.	M.B.P.M
do	30/3/17		Refill 8.45 am No T4/108185 L/Cpl OSBORNE T.S. admitted to 138 Field ambulance 1 H.D Horse No 119 evacuated from 52nd M.V.S. and struck off the strength. Weather showery	O.T.
do	31/3/17		Refill 9.10 am No T4/233814 Dr WIGGINS G. W. admitted to 138 Field ambulance. Weather Showery	O.T.

L. Griffin Lieut for Capt

WAR DIARY
or
INTELLIGENCE SUMMARY

(Erase heading not required.)

Army Form C. 2118

1 Headquarters Company
41st ~~Divisional~~ TRAIN.

Place	Date	Hour	Summary of Events and Information	Remarks and references to Appendices
RENINGHELST	1/4/17	6.95 A.M.	Refill. No. TR3 Dr. KELLY. J.J. admitted to 138 F.A. No TR3/A 3/6/17 Dr. WILSON. P.R. discharged from 138 F.A. Weather Showery	RSB
Do.	2/4/17	6.30 A.M.	Refill. No TR3 187/53 Dr. KELLY. J.J. discharged from Div Rest Station Weather Dull & mild	RSB
Do.	3/4/17	6.30 A.M.	Refill. 1 H.D. Mule killed & 3 wounded. H.Q. Shower Bt. & 3 Sects to M.V.S. Dumps	RSB
Do.	4/4/17	7.30 A.M.	Refill. 1 sick sent to M.V.S. Weather Showery	RSB
Do.	5/4/17	7.30 A.M.	Refill. No 74 233814 L. Cpl. OSBORNE T.S. wounded to C.C.S. in 2nd Inf. & Shunter Bt. charger. Weather fine	RSB
Do.	6/4/17	7.20 A.M.	Refill. No. 74 233814 Dr. WIGGINS, G.W. discharged from D.R.S. Weather fine	RSB
Do.	7/4/17	7.45 A.M.	Refill. No. 84014 060014 Cpl. TAPLIN C.L.L. appointed A/Sgt. vice Pvy from 11/4/17. Weather fine	RSB

WAR DIARY or INTELLIGENCE SUMMARY

Army Form C. 2118

41st DIVISIONAL TRAIN

Place	Date	Hour	Summary of Events and Information	Remarks and references to Appendices
RENINGHELST	8/4/17		Refill 8 A.M. 1 H.S. discharged for M.V.S. & 1 H.S. admitted to M.V.S. H.Q. Lave No. 86. died at J.I.S. through shock S/4/17. Weather 2/Cpl. Shynes giving to P.B.I. Shutes. Burst air distr 150 the RFA Rather stormy & glassing	Past B
Do	9/4/17	7.20 A.M.	Refill. Rather stormy & glassing	Past
Do	10/4/17	7.20 A.M.	Refill. Dr. WIGG 1.N.S. G.W. & No.7th 2/Cpl. SEATON. J.T. admitted to 128 E.F.A. 02313.00 Rather glassing	Past
Do	11/4/17	7.20 A.M.	Refill. 2 H.S. turn stuck to shing to shell wound Rather Fog W.E.	Past
Do	12/4/17	7.20 A.M.	Refill. Infected Piveau Pork Transport 2 A.S. were discharged for 52nd M.V.S. Rather stormy	Past
Do	13/4/17	7.45 A.M.	Refill. Rather fine	Past
Do	14/4/17	7.45 A.M.	Refill. Order discharged for M.V.S. No.Type L/Cpl. SEATON. J.G. discharged for 182 2.A. Weather fine; glassing later Rather much	Past

WAR DIARY or INTELLIGENCE SUMMARY

Army Form C. 2118

___ COMPANY 41st [Division]

Place	Date	Hour	Summary of Events and Information	Remarks and references to Appendices
REMINGHELST	15/4/17		Refile 1 - 4.5 A.M. Weather Wet.	[sgd]
Do.	16/4/17		Refile 2 - 4.5 A.M. Weather fine. No. 7860 Dr. KELLY J.J. admitted to 138th F.A.	[sgd]
Do.	17/4/17		Refile 2 - 5.5 A.M. Weather Showery. L/H.D. horses received from remounts & taken on strength.	[sgd]
Do.	18/4/17		Refile 2 - 5.0 A.M. Weather. No. 74915 Dr: Saddler KISBLE. W.W. transferred to 188 depot (H.T. 4003) as Sngler to establishment. Weather wet.	[sgd]
Do.	19/4/17		Refile 2 - 5.0 A.M. Weather Showery.	[sgd]
Do.	20/4/17		Rm I refilling at Cailleret. Changed to J. 4.5 A.H. No. 7th. 15/105 Driver KELLY. J.J. discharged from 138 F.A. Weather fine & bright.	[sgd]
Do.	21/4/17		Refile 2 - 5.0 A.M. No. 74 No. 94289 Dr: LOVELL. C. admitted to 123rd F.A. No. 15266 A/Saddler S. Sgt: STURGESS. A.C. transferred from 3rd Divisional Train. Weather fine.	[sgd]

Army Form C. 2118

WAR DIARY or INTELLIGENCE SUMMARY

(Erase heading not required.)

Headquarters COMPANY (struck through)

41st DIVISIONAL TRAIN.

Place	Date	Hour	Summary of Events and Information	Remarks and references to Appendices
RENINGHELST.	22/4/17	Reveille 5.45 A.M.	Weather fine.	Pass
Do.	23/4/17	Reveille 5.20 A.M.	No T/350/4 Dr COLGAN.J. rejoined Coy: under escort having overstayed his pass whilst in ENGLAND on 6 May 1916. No T4/034214 Dr WIGGINS.G.(W.) posted discharged from Divn. R.S. Weather fine.	Pass
Do.	24/4/17	Reveille 5.30 A.M.	Rigger & supply pokes from A.S.D. Poperinghe, 1 pole R.F.A. rejoined from Infantry. Weather fine.	Pass
Do.	25/4/17	Reveille 5.45 A.M.	Weather fine.	Pass
Do.	26/4/17	Reveille 5.45 A.M.	No 74/004299 Dr LOVELL.E. wounded to C.C.S. on 22/4/17 & struck off strength. 2 Supplies & 1 baggage wgn. 6 H.D. lorries & 2 divn. carts rejoined from R.F.A. Weather fine.	Pass
Do.	27/4/17	Reveille 5.30 A.M.	Weather fine.	Pass
Do.	28/4/17	Reveille 5.30 A.M.	Weather fine.	Pass

Army Form C. 2118

WAR DIARY
or
INTELLIGENCE SUMMARY
(Erase heading not required.)

Instructions regarding War Diaries and Intelligence Summaries are contained in F. S. Regs, Part II. and the Staff Manual respectively. Title Pages will be prepared in manuscript.

~~Headquarters~~ COMPANY
DATE ....
No. ....
41st DIVISIONAL TRAIN.

Place	Date	Hour	Summary of Events and Information	Remarks and references to Appendices
RENINGHELST	29/4/17		Rifle 5:45 A.M. 1) H.Q. Lorry (attached to D.H.Q.) died of shock of strength. Weather fine.	PS.B
Do:	30/4/17		Refill 10 A.M. Dr. E. TRIPP admitted to 138 F.A. with Overiskes. Weather fine.	PS.B

B.W. Parker, Captain
O.C. 1 ~~Headquarters~~ COY. 41ST DIVL TRAIN

1875 W. W593/826 1,000,000 4/15 J.B.C. & A. A.D.S.S./Forms/C. 2118.

Army Form C. 2118

WAR DIARY
or
INTELLIGENCE SUMMARY
(Erase heading not required.)

Instructions regarding War Diaries and Intelligence Summaries are contained in F. S. Regs., Part II. and the Staff Manual respectively. Title Pages will be prepared in manuscript.

HEAD QUARTERS COMPANY

DATE ....
No. ....

41st DIVISIONAL TRAIN.

Place	Date	Hour	Summary of Events and Information	Remarks and references to Appendices
RENINGHELST	1/5/17		Reqsple. 9. 45 A.M. No. 74573 A/L/Cpl EVANS. M. transferred from our Depot (A.T.S.)	N/A
			On 30/4/17. & taken on strength. Capt. M. B. POLLARD - URQUHART transferred to Train H.Qrs. Weather fine & hot.	
Do.	2/5/17	Refill 9. 50 A.M.	Weather fine & hot.	Refs.
Do.	3/5/17	Refill 9. 45 A.M.	Weather fine & hot.	Refs.
Do.	4/5/17	Refill 9. 50 A.M.	Weather fine & hot. Our turn in static lines during day for first time.	Refs.
Do.	5/5/17	Refill 10.20 A.M.	No.305838 Dr. WILSON. G. & 1 Order transferred to Train H.Q. Weather fine.	Refs.
Do.	6/5/17	Refill 9. 45 A.M.	Weather fine.	Refs.
Do.	7/5/17	Refill 9. 45 A.M.	Weather fine.	Refs.
Do.	8/5/17	Refill 9. 50 A.M.	No.T4/069429 Dr. LOVELL. E. rejoined from W. C.C.S. Weather fine.	Refs.
Do.	9/5/17	Refill 9. 45 A.M.	Weather fine.	Refs.

Army Form C. 2118.

HEAD QUARTERS COMPANY
41st DIVISIONAL TRAIN.

WAR DIARY
or
INTELLIGENCE SUMMARY
(Erase heading not required.)

Instructions regarding War Diaries and Intelligence Summaries are contained in F. S. Regs., Part II. and the Staff Manual respectively. Title Pages will be prepared in manuscript.

Place	Date	Hour	Summary of Events and Information	Remarks and references to Appendices
REMINGHELST	1/5/17		Refill 9.30 A.M. No 74667 Dr. Saddle JONES H. Transfered to Base Depot as suffering to establish gunshot wound. NOT/35/881 Dr. COLES. F.G. admitted to Hospital. Scabies - one	Reg.
Do.	2/5/17		Refill 9.15 A.M. 9 driving wagon + train H.Q. lorries rejoined from detachment with B. 1/30 R.F.A. Scabies - one	Reg.
Do.	10/5/17		Refill 10.12 A.M. Iwad Emp Camp, which we later gave up by 1 Coy. 223rd Div Train to Emp latchly occupied by 2 Bn. + adjoining 3 Coy + from T H.Q. line destroyed of Church St. Walker Line	M.S.
Do.	10/5/17		Refill 10.10 A.M. No 71306 Farrier Cpl. CROCKFORD F. W. sent to 2nd Army Workshop for uniform duty. Isolation one. Scabies in Stores.	Reg.

WAR DIARY or INTELLIGENCE SUMMARY

Army Form C. 2118.

HEAD QUARTERS COMPANY

41st Division Tn N.

Place	Date	Hour	Summary of Events and Information	Remarks and references to Appendices
RENINGHELST	24/5/17		Retd 10 A.M. 4 Riding horses for place- Rertd 0189 Otts RFA Army Supply.	
			No T4/015174 Dr: GODDARD. A.H. No T4/142559 Dr: MARSHALL. R. T4/094195 T1SR/01776 T2/11076 " LAWLOR. P.	
			" KERMODE. F. " SAWDFORD. A.	
			Fr. H.Q. Hy RFA.	
			No T2/36235 Dr: DAVIES. R.J. No T2/033066 Dr: RUSSELL. T. T4/065204 " CAMDEN. G.W. T1SR/36577 " WALKER. J. T1SR/02932 " COWELL. J.J.	(sd) Isabella(?) Powe

WAR DIARY
or
INTELLIGENCE SUMMARY

(Erase heading not required.)

Army Form C. 2113.

HEADQUARTERS COMPANY
41st CHYT... LOAN.

Place	Date	Hour	Summary of Events and Information	Remarks and references to Appendices
RENINGHELST	15/5/19		Rifle 10 A.M. No 74 168/85 L/Cpl OSBORNE T.S. & T/32603 Dr. SPARKS. R.A. Transferred from Muse deptr (A.S.T &S) Weather fine	WD
Do	16/5/19		Rifle D. 50 A.M. Weather showery	WD
Do	17/5/19		Rifle D. 50 A.M. No 74/120 Dr. HARPER T. transferred from No. 2 Coy; 2 divns, L.A.D lines & Q.G.S. lorry detached from detachment w/e e/15 RFA. No 1334 Q.M. HAYNES W. joined on return to Chaplain R.N.L.M. BROWNE - PtB C.E. joined this unit from 124 Bttn. Weather WD	WD
Do	18/5/19		Rifle D. 45 A.M. Weather fine	WD
Do	19/5/19		Rifle D. 50 A.M. Weather fine	WD
Do	20/5/19		Rifle 10.20 A.M. Weather fine	WD

WAR DIARY or INTELLIGENCE SUMMARY

Army Form C. 2118.

HEAD QUARTERS COMPANY
11th DIVISION

Place	Date	Hour	Summary of Events and Information	Remarks and references to Appendices
RENINGHELST	21/5/17		Reveille 5:30 A.M. Major KNOTT A.V.C. inspected horse lines & G.S. Gen. Wagon Stand To. H.S. Loss due to enemy activities not reported.	1857
Do.	22/5/17		Reveille 5:30 A.M. 2 H.S. Lorries received from Remounts 151st MT Col. G.H.Q. Weigh on 16th inst to G.E.M. for division & transferred to Army J.P. Sec. 8 No. 1 Reserve Plumery.	1857
Do.	23/5/17		Reveille 10:50 A.M. Br COLGAN. J. admitted division hospital. Reason Flu.	1857
Do.	24/5/17		Reveille 5:30 A.M. No. 16000 Br COLE P. assigned 23 days P.P. No. 1 & admitted division hospital. Reason Flu.	1857
Do.	25/5/17		Reveille changed to RENINGHELST Siding a rifle 6 A.M. & picks by H. SENDALL Temp Lt. Stayed on 24th inst as thing unfit for Active Service. Ran Fin.	1858

T.2134. Wt. W708—776. 500000. 4/15. Sir J. C. & S.

WAR DIARY
or
INTELLIGENCE SUMMARY

Army Form C. 2118.

HEAD QUARTERS COMPANY
41st DIVISIONAL TRAIN.

Place	Date	Hour	Summary of Events and Information	Remarks and references to Appendices
RENINGHELST	1.7.17	0430	Relief of Divisional G.S. Lorries & M.A.C. Lorries attached to 1st Cavalry Bde. Weather fine.	
Do.	2.7.17		Relief A.M. Lt C TRIPP returned to duty. Lt Col A.S.H. HUGHES J. Received Orders Englhad Posted to 14th Divn when to Org. Duty M.R. 2nd? Amus 2 A.D. Being occupied from Hammonds. Weather fine.	
Do	3.7.17		Relief A.M. No.3 Coy. Lt. THORPE A. Singnalls to Coy. M.C.C.S. A 15.8.17 & & Church of England. Weather fine.	
Do	4.7.17		Relief 6 A.M. Weather fine.	
Do	5.7.17		Relief 6 A.M. Lt R HARRIS reported for duty. No.2 Coy. Weather fine.	
Do	6.7.17		Received Orders to OUDERDOM "B" Echg. cooking at 3.15 A.M. Trays late owing to "B" Echg. M.R. R.GA Larder Network Ring Units to replaced. Half D. & 3/4 Amus Fire Nd. R.Q.A. Larder Network Ring Units to replaced. Reasons etc? Received from Coy. Comd. Authorised by Com. Supply & Trans.	

WAR DIARY
or
INTELLIGENCE SUMMARY.

Army Form C. 2118.

NO. 1 COMPANY,
41ST
DIVISIONAL TRAIN.

Place	Date	Hour	Summary of Events and Information	Remarks and references to Appendices
RENINGHELST	1/6/17	A.M.	Lt. R. HARRIS A.S.C. & 2/Cpl. & deleted to R Coy. No 38 Dr STEEL C.B. returned. 5 H.D. E.G.S. & 9 Shunk off Shunk Suffering from Rt. Wing 2 H.D. horses killed by Shell fire & Shunk off. 3 H.D. mules disposed of from 52 M.V.S. Weather fine.	RAB
Do.	2/6/17	A.M.	Quiet A.M. Weather fine	RAB
Do.	3/6/17	A.M.	Quiet A.M. 5 drivers & 4 H.D. & 20 H.D. mules attached from 1st Canadian Reserve Park returned to 8 Sec. 41st D.A.C. Weather fine	RAB
Do.	4/6/17	9.20 A.M.	Quiet 9.20 A.M. 1 H.D. Lorry disposed from 52nd M.V.S. 16 H.D. mules RICHARDSON M. admitted A.T.C.D.S. 005 Cgs. Weather fine	RAB
Do.	5/6/17	9.20 A.M.	Quiet 9.20 A.M. Weather fine	RAB
Do.	6/6/17	10.15 A.M.	Quiet 10.15 A.M. 1 Rider transferred to No 3 Coy. Weather fine.	RAB

WAR DIARY
or
INTELLIGENCE SUMMARY.

(Erase heading not required.)

Army Form C. 2118.

NO. 1 COMPANY,
41ST
DIVISIONAL TRAIN.

Place	Date	Hour	Summary of Events and Information	Remarks and references to Appendices
REMMGHELST	7/6/17	Retli 8 AM	Ration Strong	Post
Do	8/6/17	Reptl 8.30 AM	Ration Emé	Post
Do	9/6/17	Retli 9 AM	Ration Emé	Post
Do	10/6/17	Reptl 9 AM	J.H. & Lives discharged from M.V.S. Ration Emé	Post
Do	11/6/17	Retli 8.30 AM	2 N.S Lives received from Remount. Ration Emé	Post
Do	12/6/17	Reptl 8.15 AM	Brung Thunder Storm in Evening	Post
Do	13/6/17	Retli 7.55 AM	Coy Ordered to Move to OUDERDOM. Ration Emé	Post
OUDERDOM	14/6/17	Retli 7.50 AM	J.H. Mule (1684) died at 13th Hos. Ration Emé	Post

WAR DIARY
INTELLIGENCE SUMMARY

Army Form C. 2118.

No. 1 COMPANY, 41ST DIVISIONAL TRAIN.

Place	Date	Hour	Summary of Events and Information	Remarks and references to Appendices
OUDERDOM	15/6/17		Refill 7.30 A.M. Weather fine	RJW
Do.	16/6/17		Refill 7 A.M. No. TD.SR.0228 Dr. Oxley J. transferred to No. 4 Coy. & No. T/36036 Dr. Wilson. G. from No. 4 Coy. Weather fine	RJW
Do.	17/6/17		Refitting. Orders changed to WIPPENHOEK; refilled 7 A.M. Weather fine	RJW
Do.	18/6/17		Refilled 3 A.M. No. T/4/184704 Dr. NEEDLE. M. & No. T/4/1471 Dr. WESTON. G. & No. T/4/39230 Dr. SMITH (H.T.S.) & taker R.Sergt. Kingsbury transferred from Mob. Sec. Weather showery	RJW
Do.	19/6/17		Refilled 3 A.M. No. T/4/4375 L/Cpl EVANS. M. transferred to No. 4 Coy. Weather showery	RJW
Do.	20/6/17		Refill 3 A.M. Coy. moved from OUDERDOM at 7-30 P.M. owing to shell fire to ZEVECOTEN. Weather showery	RJW

WAR DIARY
or
INTELLIGENCE SUMMARY.
(Erase heading not required.)

Army Form C. 2118.

NO. 1 COMPANY,
41ST
DIVISIONAL TRAIN.

Place	Date	Hour	Summary of Events and Information	Remarks and references to Appendices
ZEVECOTEN	21/6/17		Rifle S.A.M. No. 74/000 Dr. COLE F. admitted to 140th Field Ambulance Isthn ISC	Red
Do.	22/6/17	8 A.M	Rifle 8 A.M. Coy: Ordered from ZEVECOTEN to Camping ground on South Side of RENINGHELST - WESTOUTRE road. Weather wet.	Red
RENINGHELST	23/6/17		Rifle 8 A.M. Coy: Arrived at Camping ground S. of ZEVECOTEN Ovile. Isthn. fine	RR
			Rifled 8 A.M. Walker fine	RR
ZEVECOTEN	24/6/17		Rifled at 3 A.M Walker fine.	RR
Do.	25/6/17		Refilled 3 A.M. 1 H.9 Rose admitted to 52nd N.V.S Walker fine	RR
Do.	26/6/17		Rifled changed to RENINGHELST Rifled 5 A.M. Isthn Skirro	RR
Do.	27/6/17		Rifle S.A.M. No 74/310 Gr MIDDLEDITCH A.H. admitted to Isfield. Walker fine	RR

WAR DIARY
or
INTELLIGENCE SUMMARY

Army Form C. 2118.

No. 1 COMPANY.
41st
DIVISIONAL TRAIN.

Place	Date	Hour	Summary of Events and Information	Remarks and references to Appendices
ZEVECOTEN	28/6/17	Refer S.A.M.	Brethren Glasbury	15/3
	29/6/17	Refer S.A.M.	Brethren Jus.	16/3
	30/6/17	Refer 4.45 A.M	Refer 10 B" S.R. Kervry - Brethren R.C.	17/3

A.B. Parker
06/10/1907 W.S.T. QMS Lieut & Major

No. 1 COMPANY.
41st
DIVISIONAL TRAIN.

Army Form C. 2118.

NO. 1 COMPANY,
41ST
DIVISIONAL TRAIN.

No. ....
Date ....

WAR DIARY
or
INTELLIGENCE SUMMARY.
(Erase heading not required.)

Instructions regarding War Diaries and Intelligence Summaries are contained in F. S. Regs, Part II. and the Staff Manual respectively. Title pages will be prepared in manuscript.

Place	Date	Hour	Summary of Events and Information	Remarks and references to Appendices
ZEVECOTEN	1/7/17		Refill S.A.A. RENINGHELST Siding. Weather fine.	App 1
Do.	2/7/17		Refill S.A.A. IHD have surrendered from M.V.S. on 27/6/17 & hand to strength. Weather fine.	App 2
Do.	3/7/17		Refill S.A.A. Weather fine.	App 3
Do.	4/7/17		Refill S.A.A. IHD. 9 horses received from Remounts & taken on strength. Weather fine.	App 4
Do.	5/7/17		Refill S.A.A. Company Cmdr'd 15 other men to SCHAECKEN. IHD have returned to Coy. 29 hrs M.V.S. & struck off strength No 174 Pte Hoggs.2.3.C 21 Cole.A.E. Seconded to 2.E.S on 26/6/17 & taken off strength. Weather fine.	App 5

T2134. Wt. W708—776. 500000. 4/15. Sir J. C. & S.

WAR DIARY
or
INTELLIGENCE SUMMARY.
(Erase heading not required.)

Army Form C. 2118.

No. 1 COMPANY,
41ST
DIVISIONAL TRAIN.

Place	Date	Hour	Summary of Events and Information	Remarks and references to Appendices
SCHAEKKEN	6/7/17		Coy. marched to Camp A. SCHAEKEN-BERTHEN road. Officer i/c Supplies between on road to Camp. D.A.C. & Sup. Column attached to No. 3 Coy. 120 Mec. R.F.A. Supplies supply attached to No. D Coy. signed supplies with 130 Field Ambulance Supply with Stables G. No. 1 Coy. Weather fine.	[illeg]
Do:	7/7/17		Refilled 2 P.M. Weather fine.	[illeg]
Do:	8/7/17		Refilled 9 P.M. No 74 Coy R.A.M.C. 168310 + 168810 Pte J. BIDDLE DITCH A.H. Evacuated to No 2 F. A. 28/6/17 + Church. Weather W.S.C.	[illeg]
Do:	9/7/17		Refilled 2 P.M. No. 566 Sergt. PHILLIPS A. & 54323 L/Cpl. RICHARDSON M. attached to Eng. Coy. to take twelve days Bomb throwing & Lewis Gun Course. Weather fine.	[illeg]

T2134. Wt. W708—776. 500000. 4/15. Sir J.C. & S.

WAR DIARY or INTELLIGENCE SUMMARY.

(Erase heading not required.)

Army Form C. 2118.

No. 1 COMPANY, 41st DIVISIONAL TRAIN.

Place	Date	Hour	Summary of Events and Information	Remarks and references to Appendices
SCHAEXKEN	10/7/17	Refill 2 P.M.	Weather fine.	13 AW
Do.	11/7/17	Refill 2 P.M.	Weather fine.	13 AW
Do.	12/7/17	Refill 11-30 A.M.	No. 72 Dr: GORTON. E. admitted to 140th F.A. Weather fine.	13 AW
Do.	13/7/17	Refill 11-20 A.M.	No. 72 Dr: GORTON. E. discharged 140th F.A. Weather fine.	13 AW
Do.	14/7/17	Refill 11-20 A.M.	Weather showery at times.	13 AW
Do.	15/7/17	Refill 11-30 A.M.	D.A.D.V.S. inspected horses & equipment, expressed satisfaction. Weather fine.	13 AW
Do.	16/7/17	Refill 11-30 A.M.	1 mule (No. 2) admitted to 52nd M.V.S. for vaccination. Weather fine.	13 AW
Do.	17/7/17	Refill 11-30 A.M.	G.O.C. inspected boys at 4-30 P.M. in drill order. Expressed satisfaction. Weather fine.	13 AW

WAR DIARY
or
INTELLIGENCE SUMMARY.

Army Form C. 2118.

No. 1 COMPANY, 41ST DIVISIONAL TRAIN.

Place	Date	Hour	Summary of Events and Information	Remarks and references to Appendices
SCHAEXKEN	18/7/17		Reveille 1-20 A.M. Weather Wet	RM
Do.	19/7/17		Reveille 11-20 A.M. 10:50/603 Dr. SPARKS R.A. admitted to 139 F.A. 1 bay. 249 took 4 of the dinner 09:30/439 Dr. MORRISON, I.S.O. opened an enquiry into 238 Snelling from Offr. Cartridges of Enquiry on 31/3/17. 1 Bundle evacuated to No 138 Fd Sketch, H G Coy H Kentachine	Rs
Do.	20/7/17		Reveille 1-30 A.M. Weather fine	RM
Do.	21/7/17		Reveille 11-20 A.M. Weather fine	RM
SCHAEXKEN	22/7/17		Reveille at SCHAEXKEN at 11-20 A.M. Company marched to Camp at REMIGHELST - LOCRE arrd. M 5. C. 20. Sheet 28 . Weather fine	RM
ZEVCOTEN				
ZEVCOTEN	23/7/17		Reveille 1-20 P.M. Sir Suff Comm Bushenden Inspn by H. PARKER Asst. over Company Comm and Suff Guin Ohey Inspection of Li Lt. Col. MOLONY.	RM

T2134. Wt. W708-776. 500000. 4/15. Sir J. C. & S.

WAR DIARY
or
INTELLIGENCE SUMMARY
(Erase heading not required.)

Army Form C. 2118.

NO. 1 COMPANY,
41ST DIVISIONAL TRAIN.

No. ....
Date ....

Instructions regarding War Diaries and Intelligence Summaries are contained in F.S. Regs., Part II. and the Staff Manual respectively. Title pages will be prepared in manuscript.

Place	Date	Hour	Summary of Events and Information	Remarks and references to Appendices
ZEVECOTEN	24/7/17		Refill 1.30 P.M. as 20ᵗʰ Inf. Bᵈᵉ 52 SR Pte WINTON J.E. 01763 Admitted B 140ᵗʰ F.A. Butter fine	MWB
Do.	25/7/17		Refill from Railhead at BRULOOSE at 9.20 A.M. Talk refilling details as 20ᵗʰ Inf Bᵈᵉ No. 7 Sr. S. PARKS R.A. ditched 2nd 140ᵗʰ F.A. 1 Mule 325 wounded to M.V.S. Butter fine.	MWB
Do.	26/7/17		Refill as usual 9.20 A.M. Butter fine.	MWB
Do.	27/7/17		Refill as usual 9.20 A.M. Gunner killed by shell Gr & 3 H.Q. Lorry swamped, all stores 187763 Dr. CULLEN P. drowned to Spl. fire. Returned 187 F.A. 1 rider T.P.W. PROCKTER AK. as 14ᵗʰ Inf Brde and of Train. Butter fine.	MWB
Do.	28/7/17		Refill 9.20 A.M. Butter fine.	MWB

WAR DIARY
or
INTELLIGENCE SUMMARY

Army Form C. 2118.

Place	Date	Hour	Summary of Events and Information	Remarks and references to Appendices
ZEVECOTEN	29/7/19	9.20 A.M.	Brake Set.	
Do.	30/7/19	9.20 A.M.	Refill. Also Lnn. A.E. & Th. Pts. Transferred from Post 14 Regd. (at 9.5) Back W.P.22065 Pte. WHITE. A.	
Do.	31/7/19	9.20 A.M.	Refill. Brake fine	

O.C. 1 Coy 41st Divisional Train

WAR DIARY or INTELLIGENCE SUMMARY

Army Form C. 2118.

No. 1 COMPANY, 41ST DIVISIONAL TRAIN.

Place	Date	Hour	Summary of Events and Information	Remarks and references to Appendices
2 ELCBERG	1/9/17		Rifle at Hand 9.20 A.M. Shelter Vary 1.S.C.	AS8
Do.	2/9/17	9.20 A.M.	Refug 9.20 A.M. No. 1 Dr. CULLEN.P. evacuated to 41st C.C.S. A.29/8/17. Suffering from shrapnel wound of thigh & shock. 2nd Lt. E. Dr. E. LUFF transferred from No. 2 Coy. Shelter W.S.C.	AS8
Do.	3/9/17	9.20 A.M.	Refile 9.20 A.M. 6 dumps & lorry 9 to AD dump detached to 206 Field Coy R.E. Shelter W.S.C.	AS8
Do.	4/9/17	9.20 A.M.	Refile 9.20 A.M. No. 74 Dr. WIGGINS.G.W. killed by shell fire nr early R.E. dump in the vicinity of SAM STRASSE. Buried Sr. LA CLYTTE Military cemetery. Sheet 28. N.2.6.39. Sheet 36 S.W. (Belgium & France. New Edition) Sr. ANDREWS.D.E. Dr. RULE Edgar (14 + 18) taken to Chiug. No. 38 Sr. COLGAN.J. Wpr. Wall A.37.8 C.C.S. Dr. McCluskey John Reynolds 9/5 Aing to 1A Dump & lorry 1 supt & 1 light detached to 233 Field Coy R.E. for load after lying etc. etc. 2 orders. Shelter W.S.C.	AS8

WAR DIARY
or
INTELLIGENCE SUMMARY.

(Erase heading not required.)

Army Form C. 2118.

NO. 1 COMPANY.
41ST
DIVISIONAL TRAIN.

Place	Date	Hour	Summary of Events and Information	Remarks and references to Appendices
ZEYCOTEN	5/5/17	9.20 AM	Rifle & Leather drill.	Nil
Do.	6/5/17		Railhead. Altered to BAILLEUL 9.45 AM (J: 74) YOUNG. T. from Bark depôt (J 35) & take to Détails D.22 the Gue.	Nil
Do.	7/5/17		Rifle & 9.30 AM 4 do 6.5 HC (0.70.4) Sir Corgan admitted to 35th C.C.S. on 4th inst. A Shnell 55th Shent B. No: 75422 Sergent HAMILTON A. Attacked & Smirked 13.S. Self-inflicted 9047. Gun. 1 AD muk Scounded Gunshot 10.S.S. right augerine 4650 Shell. Gue.	Nil
Do.	8/5/17	8.45 AM	Rifle & AJA at BAILLEUL taking 2 buyer & hagger No 129 home of Winchester to DCM Died by Rt Rev Monag & Cap: Servard of the Ruve Returned with wagons. Leather Gue.	Nil
Do.	9/5/17	9.30 AM	Rifle at BAILLEUL (No 74) W. Q.M.G. Div. Supply Inspected Carts attached for from (J 45) by D.W.S. Gue. Occurred to them un Leather Gue.	Nil
Do.	10/5/17		Rifle & Kit inspection. Driving drees & Kit. All in order. Leather Que.	Nil

WAR DIARY or INTELLIGENCE SUMMARY

Army Form C. 2118.

NO. 1 COMPANY, 41ST DIVISIONAL TRAIN.

Place	Date	Hour	Summary of Events and Information	Remarks and references to Appendices
ZEVECOTEN	10/8/17		Reveille 5.30 AM as usual. (Details to hourly) returned to Company from issue out duty. Weather fine.	RB
Do.	11/8/17		Routine work (as task) BRULOOZE Section Working and (wounded on duty info)	RB
Do.	12/8/17		Reveille 10.15 AM. No. 1-2-3-4 Sub Sections PROVEN Section HQ + Salm Ch 295627 Sheet 28. HQ ADS Coy + 1 field Ambulance No. 2.3.3 Field Companies R.E. 15-16AM JAD/Coy. Loaned 5 lorries at S. Ingm for detachment not feeding.	RB
Do.	13/8/17		Reveille 4.45 AM. Weather fine.	RB
Do.	14/8/17		Reveille 10-15 AM. D.E. 1mm Wheeled Camb to Company I.G.S wagon received from ADS to replace one destroyed by shell fire on 7/8/17.	RB

T2134. Wt. W708—776. 500000. 4/15. Sir J. C. & S.

WAR DIARY
or
INTELLIGENCE SUMMARY

Army Form C. 2118.

No. 1 COMPANY,
41ST
DIVISIONAL TRAIN.

Place	Date	Hour	Summary of Events and Information	Remarks and references to Appendices
ZEVCOTEN	15/5/17		Refill as usual. Divisional Amm. Park moved to new area with division, leaving No. 1 Company with 3rd Artillery. Weather showery.	MJB
Do	16/5/17		Refill as usual. Weather fine.	MJB
Do	17/5/17		Refill at 3.45 A.M. Army of light draught handed over to No. 3 Coy for O.R. re-issue to units. Weather fine.	MJB
Do	18/5/17		Refill @ 4.15 A.M. 2.A.D. horses received from Armentières. Weather fine.	MJB
Do	19/5/17		Refill @ 4.15 A.M. Weather fine.	MJB
Do	20/5/17		Refill @ 4.15 A.M. Weather fine.	MJB

WAR DIARY
INTELLIGENCE SUMMARY
(Erase heading not required.)

Army Form C. 2118.

No. 1 COMPANY,
41st
DIVISIONAL TRAIN.

Place	Date	Hour	Summary of Events and Information	Remarks and references to Appendices
ZEVECOTEN	21/6/17		Refill as usual at 10 A.M. Weather fine.	PSW
Do	22/6/17		Refill at 9.45 A.M. Weather fine.	PSW
Do	23/6/17		Capt W. Tite of Guildford. Supplies drawn from train at 9 PM. Refill as usual. Weather fine.	PSW
Do	24/6/17		Refill at usual 9.45 A.M. Supplies before A.S.C. Batteries & Refill H.Q. of 190 R.F.A. drawn from train usual 6 P.M.	
Do	25/6/17		Refill as usual. Supply wagon of A.S.C. Column & Refill to Rgt. R.F.A. proceeded to LOCRE after staying in Suffolk. Weather fine.	PSW
Do	26/6/17		Refill as usual. Weather fine.	PSW

Army Form C. 2118.

NO. 1 COMPANY.
41ST
DIVISIONAL TRAIN.
No.: ....
Date: ....

WAR DIARY
or
INTELLIGENCE SUMMARY.
(Erase heading not required.)

Instructions regarding War Diaries and Intelligence Summaries are contained in F.S. Regs., Part II. and the Staff Manual respectively. Title pages will be prepared in manuscript.

Place	Date	Hour	Summary of Events and Information	Remarks and references to Appendices
2 EVESTER	27/8/17	Refill 9.45 a.m.	1 H D horse No.109 lost on 28th July 17 struck off the strength authority 2nd Army/u 8/2650/12 cratus 22.8.17 and in its steaven No 917/12 dated 24.8.17. Weather wet	W.T.
do	28.8.17	Refill 9.45 a.m.	No T4/043499 Pyt & No T4/211386 a/Sgt MORTIMER S.E. & No T4/039938 L. BRADLEY F.C. transferred from Base depot and taken on the strength, weather showery	W.T.
do	29.8.17	Refill 9.45 a.m.	1 H D horse No 126 destroyed, weather showery	W.T.
do	30.8.17	Refill 9.45 a.m.	Weather fine	W.T.
do	31.8.17	Refill 9.45 a.m.	Weather fine	W.T.

for O.C. No. 1 Coy. 41st Div. Train

WAR DIARY
INTELLIGENCE SUMMARY.
(Erase heading not required.)

Army Form C. 2118.

Place	Date	Hour	Summary of Events and Information	Remarks and references to Appendices
ZEVECOTEN	1.9.17		Refill 2 p.m. I H Dhorse admitted to 50 M.V.S. Weather showery	le. ?
	2.9.17		Company moved at 10.30 p.m. ZEVECOTEN to camp on BUESCHERE-ABEELE Road (Sheet 27 S.E.) R.3.c.y. I H Dhorse 6.15 p.m. Refill 6.15 p.m. I H Dhorse M 60 attached to No 4 Coy train was evacuated on I.O.M. and struck off the strength. Weather fine	le. ?
BOESCHERE	3.9.17		Refill by motor lorries at 5.30 p.m. Weather fine	le. ?
"	4.9.17		Refill at 4 p.m. Weather fine	le. ?
"	5.9.17		Refill at 1.30 p.m. Weather fine	le. ?
"	6.9.17		Refill at 10 p.m. Weather fine	le. ?
"	7.9.17		Refilled twice at 12.30 P.M. & 9.5 P.M. No: 74733 Dr. NEWTON.S. admitted 17.9.17 to 130 Field Ambulance as 2° n.y.d. Weather fine.	le. ?

Army Form C. 2118.

No. 1 COMPANY,
41ST
DIVISIONAL TRAIN.

WAR DIARY
or
INTELLIGENCE SUMMARY.
(Erase heading not required.)

Instructions regarding War Diaries and Intelligence Summaries are contained in F. S. Regs., Part II. and the Staff Manual respectively. Title pages will be prepared in manuscript.

Place	Date	Hour	Summary of Events and Information	Remarks and references to Appendices
BOESCHEPE	8/9/17		Refill 3 P.M. Bulthe Sine.	P.B.S.
Do.	9/9/17		Refill 8 P.M. No. T4H Dr. FROGGATT. A.W.J. admitted to 188 Field Ambulances Bulthe Sine.	P.B.S.
Do.	10/9/17		Refill 2.30 P.M. No. T4/88 Dr. NEWTON. S. Wounded to M.R. C.C.S. on 9.9.17 not on strength Bulther Line.	P.B.S.
Do.	11/9/17		Refill 8.30 P.M. No. T4/313 Gr. WHITE. A.R.M. admitted to 138 F.A. 10/9/17 Bulther Line.	P.B.S.
do. & ZEVECOTEN	12/9/17		Refill from Line at ZEVECOTEN at 8 P.M. Company marched from BOESCHEPE to ZEVECOTEN. HURON Camp M.5.23.9.0 Bulther Line.	P.B.S.
ZEVECOTEN	13/9/17		Refill 8 P.M. from Lorries Bulther Line & edde; Crew at Anytime	P.B.S.

T2134. Wt. W708—776. 500000. 4/15. Sir J. C. & S.

WAR DIARY
or
INTELLIGENCE SUMMARY

Army Form C. 2118.

No. 1 COMPANY.
41ST DIVISIONAL TRAIN.

Place	Date	Hour	Summary of Events and Information	Remarks and references to Appendices
2 EYKE STN.	14/3/17		Rehle at railway BRVL-002 E. at 11.30 A.M. 60 British Infty signed 2 A.S. hopes & 2 F.S. Ambry received. Rations for Br: 10 F. Bdr: & D.A.C. 16 Emplys: 161 Brigade Hdqrs: Newton S. Arty. organised from 2 C.S. on 10 F.BMRS. 1st Division Train	Arg1
Do.	15/3/17		Rehle 11.30 A.M. 61st Infty Bd railway Evacuated 1 H.Q. 61st Infty Bd. 1st Division Train	Arg.
Do.	16/3/17		Rehle at 9.30 A.M. & 5.30 P.M.V.S Evacuated. 1 H.Q. Infty 16.75 & 11 Div. Uncle Jas. Newton, A.W. J. Evacuated to C.C.S. on 7/5/64 Br: FROGGATT No. 20/6/01 Pte HUDSON J. (Gdns) Evacuated to C.C.S. on 5/15 Inst: 4 Kinch M. 1st Division Train	158
Do.	17/3/17		Rehle 2.30 P.M. 190 Mgle RFA Arrived at OUDER D.M Sinkhead Infty 11/15 Div. N.S.* 16: HAINSWORTH A.E. (115) Transferred from Chtz. Depot 1st Division Train	N.S.B.

T2131. Wt. W708—776. 500000. 4/15. Sir J. C. & S.

WAR DIARY
or
INTELLIGENCE SUMMARY.

(Erase heading not required.)

Army Form C. 2118.

No. 1 COMPANY.
41st
DIVISIONAL TRAIN.

Place	Date	Hour	Summary of Events and Information	Remarks and references to Appendices
2EYCOTE N.18	18/9/17	10.30 AM	Refill Bruloozeele. Weather fine.	Post
Do.	19/9/17.	9.50 AM	Refill D.50 A.M. Major R.D.L.W. G.A. transferred to Ammn. Park. No.34/8647/84 A.M. G.S. Infantry. 0647/84. Weather fine.	Post
Do.	20/9/17.	8.30	Refill 8.30 Bruloozeele 9-50 OUDERDOM. Weather fine.	Post
Do.	21/9/17.	9.45 AM	All supplies today refilled with H.P. Ousnn at OUDERDOM. Arrived 9.45 A.M. Weather fine.	Post
Do.	22/9/17.	9/15 AM	Refill at 9/15 A.M. D.H.S. Ins. No.74. watered at R.E.C.G. on 20 inst. 91/310 Pte WHITE. A.R.H. Weather fine.	Post
Do.	23/9/17.	9.45 AM	Refill 9.45 A.M. 1 H.D. Junk. St 1 Mule drowned at D.E. Inst. St. Weather fine.	Post

WAR DIARY
or
INTELLIGENCE SUMMARY.

(Erase heading not required.)

Army Form C. 2118.

No. 1 COMPANY,
41ST
DIVISIONAL TRAIN.

Place	Date	Hour	Summary of Events and Information	Remarks and references to Appendices
ZEYCOTEN	24/9/17		Rifle 11.30 A.M. at RENINGHELST filling into 39th Division. Weather fine.	1035
Do.	25/9/17		Rifle 8.40 A.M. at OUDERDOM with 39th Division. Weather fine.	1035
Do.	26/9/17		Rifle 8.40 A.M. at Do. 39th Div. Weather fine.	1035
Do.	27/9/17		Rifle 8 A.M. at Do. 39th Div. Weather fine.	1035
Do.	28/9/17		Rifle 6.45 A.M. at Do. 39th Div. Weather fine.	1035
Do.	29/9/17		Rifle 8.45 A.M. Ed. School. Weather fine.	1035
Do.	30/9/17		Refill 7.30 A.M. with 31st Div. Sec 182 Bgd R.F.A. and 6 SCHAERKEN area with supply of Regt & wgn. Weather fine.	1035

M. Gallagher, Major, A.S.C.
O.C. 1 Coy. 41st Div. Train.

WAR DIARY or **INTELLIGENCE SUMMARY**

Army Form C. 2118.

No. 1 COMPANY. 41st DIVISIONAL TRAIN.

Place	Date	Hour	Summary of Events and Information	Remarks and references to Appendices
ZEVECOTEN	1/10/17		Refill Ordered 9.30 A.M. W+ Dist Supply No. T59 Stringer J.E. Dist Bakery No1109 Dr. Satchell W. + No. T59 F10308 Dr. Stringer J.E. Dist Bakery posting fur Dyte A/Cpl to D.S.A/7 + 10308 Taken on Stengh. No. T4/248 Dr. Bowman R. admitted to 20/2 F.A. Weather fine.	(Sd)
Do.	2/10/17		Refill 10 A.M. No 1. No. T4/266 Dr. Hurren A. admitted to 22 F.A. Weather fine.	(Sd)
Do.	3/10/17		Refill as usual. Weather fine; some rain.	(Sd)
Do.	4/10/17		Refill 8.30 A.M. as usual. No. T4/248 Dr. Bowman R. discharged from 22d F.A. Weather fine.	(Sd)
Do.	5/10/17		Refill 8.30 A.M. No T4/33 Sgt Leslie A.G. & 1 riding horse transferred to 188 A.F.A. Bgde. Weather Stormy.	(Sd)

WAR DIARY or INTELLIGENCE SUMMARY

Army Form C. 2118.

No. 1 COMPANY, 41ST DIVISIONAL TRAIN.

Place	Date	Hour	Summary of Events and Information	Remarks and references to Appendices
ZEGGERS-CAPPEL	1/10/17		Refill of March. No. 74/56 Pte HURREN. N.A. discharged from 22nd F.A. to this Company.	App 8
Do.	2/10/17		Company agreed to send S.A.M. ZERMEZEELE, leaving S.A.M. arrived 3 P.M. Delivered supplies to units & arrived & refilled by 1st.	App 8
ZERMEZEELE	3/10/17		Company arrived at 7 A.M. to S.C. POL-SUR-MARE arriving 1.15 P.M. Delivered supplies on arrival & refilled 2 A.S.C. Lorries 56D Echeloned to S.2nd M.V.S. for No. 9 Coy. Weather fine.	App 8
ST POL SUR MARE	9/10/17		Refill from lorries. Weather fine.	App
Do.	10/10/17		Refill & & Do. Weather fine.	App 8
Do.	11/10/17		Supplies drawn from railhead by Park transport 8.30 A.M. No.73/93 Pte COLLINS G. from 3rd Do. No. T/65 Do. STRINGER. J.E. & S/49 & No. T/65 Do. Collins G. from 3rd Coy. 3rd Do. Weather fine.	App 8

WAR DIARY
or
INTELLIGENCE SUMMARY.

(Erase heading not required.)

Army Form C. 2118.

No. 1 COMPANY,
41ST
DIVISIONAL TRAIN.

Place	Date	Hour	Summary of Events and Information	Remarks and references to Appendices
ST. POL.	12/10/17		Refld as in 11th Inst. Weather Showery	758
Do.	13/10/17		Refld Supply 115th Inf Bde 2 H.Q. & 1 L.D. occasional from Reserves in B.P. & taken in Strength. Weather fair.	158B
ST. POL. BASE	14/10/17		Company draw K St. Does BAD at V.A.H. arriving 9.15. declared supplies & refilled as usual. 130 Pdy Wagons Remained at ST Pol. Droc V.A.H. for L/Cpl Winterly No. T4/1000 Dr HARVEY E. for Mich H.Q & No. T4/11G St SOT CHELL 0834 W. 15 train A.Q. leaving 9/19.0 Weather fine.	158B
Do	15/10/17		Refld as in 15th Inst. Weather fine.	158B
Do	15/10/17		Refld as usual. Weather fine.	158B

WAR DIARY
or
INTELLIGENCE SUMMARY

Army Form C. 2118.

No. 1 COMPANY,
41ST DIVISIONAL TRAIN.

Place	Date	Hour	Summary of Events and Information	Remarks and references to Appendices
ST. I-ESQUAL	18/10/17		Refill as usual. 1 G.S. Wgn & 9 pairs to divnl. Switched to 41st Divnl Wing. Baker gone.	
Do	19/10/17		Refill as usual. Baker gone.	
Do	20/10/17		Refill as usual. Baker gone.	
Do	21/10/17		Refill as usual. Baker gone. 10:30 a.a/Cpl Smith G. transferred from Coy to H.Q Staff	
Do	22/10/17		Refill as usual. 2 A.S. troops & 1 aux transferred to 52 Divn. troops	
Do	23/10/17		Refill as usual. Baker gone	
Do	24/10/17		Refill as usual. The 2 A.S. lines & 1 aux & 1 cycle returned to A.V.S. 2 A.S. seconded for employ & taken on strength. A transferred from No 3 Coy. Baker gone.	

WAR DIARY
or
INTELLIGENCE SUMMARY.
(Erase heading not required.)

Army Form C. 2118.

No. 1 COMPANY,
41st
DIVISIONAL TRAIN.

Instructions regarding War Diaries and Intelligence Summaries are contained in F. S. Regs., Part II. and the Staff Manual respectively. Title pages will be prepared in manuscript.

Place	Date	Hour	Summary of Events and Information	Remarks and references to Appendices
ST. IDESBALD	25/10/17		Refill of 2 D.A.D. units. Weather fine.	
Do.	26/10/17		Refill of 2 D.A.D. units. Weather fine.	
Do.	27/10/17		Refill of Rend. Weather fine.	
Do.	28/10/17		Refill of Rend. Weather fine.	
GHYVELDE	29/10/17		Refill of Rend. Company moved to GHYVELDE 12·15 P.M. arrived 5·15 P.M. 2 A.S. Lorries Nos 648 & 649 detailed to 6·2 M.V.S. Weather fine.	
Do.	30/10/17		Received B.A.M. at ST. IDESBALD. Brother ISK No 13794 Pte HAYLES W. attached from 32 R.F. to Reuland in English Hospital admitted to Large rest station. Brother NCO.	
Do.	31/10/17		Marched out 8·30 AM for LEFFRINCKOUCKE. Weather fine	

R Shuter Major
O.C. No. 1 Co. Coy 41st Divl. Train

WAR DIARY
or
INTELLIGENCE SUMMARY

Army Form C. 2118.

No. 1 COMPANY.
41st
DIVISIONAL TRAIN.

Place	Date	Hour	Summary of Events and Information	Remarks and references to Appendices
VALLA	1/3/18		Retd from M.T. Valla Church 9-30 A.M. 2nd Lt F.L. BOOTH Kingsway to 2nd Div Train ASC pending appointment to Corps Tractor Sec.	BSM
Do	2/3/18		Refile as My 1st inst: No 7097 Pte WHITESIDE.W. reported from E.C.S. on 1st inst. (having been struck off Strength 26/10/17. No 54 04/11/13 JENKINS.W.S. & No 74 9 Pte SMITH.W.E. & 1897 Pte Skeels L/C RICHARDS.E. evacuated to E.C.S on 25/2/18. Sick 28/2/18	BSM
Do	3/3/18		Refile as on 1st inst: No 79 Driver 8611 Pte BRIDE.R. rejoined from 24 C.C.S. No 85 Corporal WHYTE.D. 3 admitted to 24 C.C.S. Weather fine	BSM
Do	4/3/18		Refile as on 1st inst: Weather very DAY	BSM
PAESE	5/3/18		Refile at VALLA as on 4th Inst: Company ordered to march over to PAESE. Weather fine.	BSM

T2134. Wt. W708—776. 500000. 4/15. Sir J. C. & S.

WAR DIARY
or
INTELLIGENCE SUMMARY

Army Form C. 2118.

No. 1 COMPANY.
41st
DIVISIONAL TRAIN.

Place	Date	Hour	Summary of Events and Information	Remarks and references to Appendices
QAGG.	6/3/16		Rifle fire at QAGG Ranch 10.20 AM to 2 AM. 545 PM Route March W.C.	Appx
Do.	7/3/16		Rifle firing at 9.20 P.M. H. E. V. GREY transferred to No 2 Section. 35 other OR's awaiting transfer to train at TREVISO.	Appx
Do.	8/3/16		Who ashife this day No: 55/193 Pte WHYTE. J discharged from H4 Ft. CS. leaves gone.	
Do.	9/3/16		Church services at TREVISO. 11.30 AM. Return of troops 5 P.M. day drawn in sick away. Batch fire.	Appx
			To B 11-9 P.M. in Rain. Cased Glass - punch sisters to night.	Appx
			10 B M.T. leaves due during evening.	
DOULLENS	15/3/16		Coy Coy detrained at Smelling 2 A.M. march to camp at ARRSSNS.	Appx
			Route via BEAUREPAIRE. Weather fine.	

WAR DIARY
or
INTELLIGENCE SUMMARY.
(Erase heading not required.)

Army Form C. 2118.

No. 1 COMPANY,
41st
DIVISIONAL TRAIN.

Instructions regarding War Diaries and Intelligence Summaries are contained in F. S. Regs., Part II. and the Staff Manual respectively. Title pages will be prepared in manuscript.

Place	Date	Hour	Summary of Events and Information	Remarks and references to Appendices
BEAUREPAIRE FM			Refill at 12 A.M. O-an Coy Gen Emp No 7572 Pte Crawford F to No 1 Coy, No: 7268 Dr. KEEPING A from No 1 Coy. No: 7495 Dr. KEEPING A to A.S.C Base Dpt. Dr COTTON? to No 1 Coy. Weather fine	A/S
Do	15/3/18		Refill 12 A.M. 14th Inf. Weather fine	B
Do	16/3/18		Refill up to 14th Inf. No: 7472 Dr. GORTON E Invalided to 2nd E.M.Dt. Bn. of Shrapnel. No: 201559 Pte LAZENBY E Invalided to C.C.S. No 20(9)R of Shrapnel. No 20/9R of Shiner W Shingle. Weather fine	C
Do	17/3/18		Refill 12 A.M. 14th Inf. Weather fine	Snow
Do-	18.3.18		Refilled at 10 P.M. also at 5.30 P.M. One H.D admitted to 52nd M.V.S. mumps. Snow	Snow
-Do-	19.3.18		Refill at 1.30 P.M. No 1/23419 Dr. Skelton E. transferred to No 2 Coy. Weather wet	Snow

Army Form C. 2118.

No. 1 COMPANY,
41st
DIVISIONAL TRAIN.

WAR DIARY
or
INTELLIGENCE SUMMARY.
(Erase heading not required.)

Instructions regarding War Diaries and Intelligence Summaries are contained in F. S. Regs., Part II. and the Staff Manual respectively. Title pages will be prepared in manuscript.

Place	Date	Hour	Summary of Events and Information	Remarks and references to Appendices
BEAUREPAIRE	20/6/18		Refilled at 1.20 p.m. Weather fine.	Enel
BAVELINCOURT	21/6/18		The Coy moved to billet at BAVELINCOURT. Supplied men delivered to units & refill took place in the village at 8 p.m. Weather fine.	Enel
ACHIET-LE-PETIT	22/6/18		Coy moved to Camp on the ACHIET-LE-PETIT — ACHIET-LE-GRAND road. No refill took place. Weather fine.	Enel
— Do —	23/6/18		Refilled on ACHIET-LE-PETIT — BUCQUOY road at midday. Our H.Q. evacuated & struck off strength. Weather fine.	Enel
— Do —	24/6/18		Refilled in Camp. Camp was shelled one G.S. wagon was completely destroyed & No. T4/094192 Dr Bridson R.D. was wounded & admitted to 138th F.A. The Coy moved to a field on the ACHIET-LE-PETIT BUCQUOY Rd. a storm to about 10 all night. No. S/335575 PTE HAINSWORTH. A.E. was transferred to Base Depot HAVRE. Weather fine.	Enel

T134. Wt. W708—776. 500000. 4/15. Sir J. C. & S.

WAR DIARY
or
INTELLIGENCE SUMMARY

Army Form C. 2118.

No. 1 COMPANY,
41st DIVISIONAL TRAIN.

Place	Date	Hour	Summary of Events and Information	Remarks and references to Appendices
ST AMAND	25/2/18		The Coy moved to St AMAND. No refit took place. Supplies were dumped in a field on the GOMMECOURT—FONQUEVILLERS road were picked up by the units. Weather fine.	Fine
BAILLEULMONT	26/2/18		Refilled at St AMAND on the St AMAND—GAUDIEMPRÉ Rd. & the Coy marched to a field off the DOULLENS—ARRAS Rd on the road to BAILLEULMONT. Weather fine.	Fine
— Do —	27/2/18		Refilled in Camp. Delivered Supplies to the Coy stood to awaiting orders. Weather fine. 2 H.D. admitted to 52nd M.V.S.	Fine
HUMBERCAMP	28/2/18		The Coy marched to HUMBERCAMP when it arrived at 2 AM & camped in a field just outside the village on the HUMBERCAMP—POMMIER Rd. Refilled in Camp about 5 pm. & supplies were delivered to units. Weather wet.	Fine
— Do —	29/2/18		Refilled at 10 A.m. Same place. No rain. Weather cloudy.	Fine
— Do —	30/2/18		Refilled at 7.30 A.m. Same place. Weather wet.	Fine
— Do —	2/3/18		Refilled at 12.20 A.m. Same place. Showery weather.	Fine

Fulwood. Capt.
for O.C. 1 Coy 41st Divisional Train.

Army Form C. 2118.

No. 1 COMPANY,
41ST
DIVISIONAL TRAIN.

WAR DIARY
or
INTELLIGENCE SUMMARY
(Erase heading not required.)

Instructions regarding War Diaries and Intelligence
Summaries are contained in F. S. Regs., Part II.
and the Staff Manual respectively. Title Pages
will be prepared in manuscript.

Place	Date	Hour	Summary of Events and Information	Remarks and references to Appendices
HUMBERCAMP	1/4/18		Refilled at 7 p.m. Weather fine	Signed
HENU	2/4/18		The Coy moved to a field outside HENU on the HENU – SOUASTRE Road. Refilled at 5 p.m. Weather fine.	Signed
– Do –	3/4/18		Refilled at 6 p.m. Weather cold & cloudy.	Signed
– Do –	4/4/18		Refilled at 3 p.m. Weather wet.	Signed
– Do –	5/4/18		Refilled at 8 p.m. Weather wet.	Signed
– Do –	6/4/18		Refilled at 8 p.m. No rain today!	Signed
Do.	7/4/18		Refill 6 P.m. Weather wet.	Signed
Do.	8/4/18		Refill 6-15 P.m. No: 344673 Sgt BARKER. G.A. admitted to hospital. Weather very wet.	Signed
Do.	9/4/18		Refill 8 P.m. Weather fine.	Signed
Do.	10/4/18		Refill 8 P.m. Weather fine.	Signed
Do.	11/4/18		Refill 4 P.m. Weather fine.	Signed
Do.	12/4/18		Refill 4 P.m. Left camp HENU. Coy moved to camp N.W. of COUIN. Weather fine.	Signed
COUIN.	13/4/18		Refill 5 Coy Camp 8.20 P.m. Weather dull & very windy.	Signed

WAR DIARY
or
INTELLIGENCE SUMMARY.
(Erase heading not required.)

Army Form C. 2118.

No. 1 COMPANY,
41ST
DIVISIONAL TRAIN.

Place	Date	Hour	Summary of Events and Information	Remarks and references to Appendices
COUIN	14/4/18		Reflg: 6½". No. 694 192 Dr. BENSON. R.D. wounded to 24/3F.A. & struck off Strength from Roll Date No. 24/3F.A. Dr. WADSWORTH.S reported to Coy. Offr. 13/4/18. Struck off Strength from Roll G.S. 2ND Line wounded 12/4/18 & Died of Wounds. London Purking Home Nyt Wait	[illegible]
Do	15/4/18		Reflg. to KENIwal army place at 4.12th Dr. No 74/52 Dr. GOLDSWORTHY. A admitted to Hospital. Lumbar. Gun	[illegible]
Do	16/4/18		Reflg. 8 a.m. to no.15 Casualty Clearing Station attached to R.F.A. and injured Shoulder & arm	[illegible]
Do	17/4/18		Reflg. 10-30 P.H. No: 74806 Dr. CROCKER. S.J. Reports attached No. 2 Coy killed by shrapnel fire. No: 57702 Dr. MITCHELL trampled S.A.D. Left arm admitted to 30 M.S. a 18 B Det. No. T44253 Driver McCOMLY. C.E. admitted to 30 M.S. + transferred to 15/4/18. Weather fine	[illegible]

WAR DIARY
or
INTELLIGENCE SUMMARY
(Erase heading not required.)

Army Form C. 2118.

Place	Date	Hour	Summary of Events and Information	Remarks and references to Appendices
COLIN	18/4/16		Return 20 Rn. the Shing transferred to Army Depot of auxiliary M.G. School 23/4/16. L.A. Shenkes 4 G.S. Lorries and No. 74101 Pt. NEWAY, H. Jnr. 2 Coy. No. 7222 Pt. BAKER W. Jnr. 4 Coy. " 245705 " ANDREWS, G.F. Jnr. 3 Coy. " HOUSTON, J. " " 888/05 " and 16114 Pte. KIDNEY, G. Jnr. 2 Coy. B 106957 Pte. COPPING R. Jnr. 2 Coy. 410. 201663 Pte. NEWALL, J. Jnr. 1 Coy. order sent to Lt. Col 4/4/16 Shells during Test.	App
Do	19/4/16		Return to Camp R. & Rh. No. 20166 Pte. TAYLOR E. admitted to 3/2nd Inspec F.A. Shelling of Bonne Shell	App
Do	20/4/16		Return to A.D.S. No. 201723 Pte. TOOLAN M. admitted 2/2nd Inspec F.A. D.A.H. Return to Linden admitted of M.V.S. Styria, Sickness of Int.	App
Do	21/4/16		Return to A.D.S. Nothing from	App
Do	22/4/16		Return to A.D.S. No. 75/343 Pte. Mc MAHER P admitted 2/2nd Inspec F.A. Shell from	App

Army Form C. 2118.

No. 1 COMPANY.
41ST
DIVISIONAL TRAIN.

WAR DIARY
or
INTELLIGENCE SUMMARY.
(Erase heading not required.)

Instructions regarding War Diaries and Intelligence Summaries are contained in F. S. Regs., Part II. and the Staff Manual respectively. Title pages will be prepared in manuscript.

Place	Date	Hour	Summary of Events and Information	Remarks and references to Appendices
COUIN	23/4/18	Refill 2 P.M.	No: 791497 Dr. GOLDSWORTHY A. transfd K.E.C.S. a. 18/4/18 & struck off strength. Weather fine.	
Do.	24/4/18	Refill 5 P.M.	Weather fine.	
Do	25/4/18	Refill 2 P.M.	Weather Showery.	
Do	26/4/18	Refill 5 P.M.	No: 36210 Dr: HAMPSTEAD H. attached from R.F.A. admitted to 139 F. Amb: L. A. on posting & struck off R.O.S. Yr. 2 f.S. Weather fine.	
Do	27/4/18	Refill 2 P.M.	Weather Showery.	
Do	28/4/18	Refill 2 P.M.	Weather Showery.	
Do	29/4/18	Refill 2 P.M.	Weather fine.	
Do	30/4/18	Refill 2 P.M.	Weather fine.	

WAR DIARY
or
INTELLIGENCE SUMMARY.
(Erase heading not required.)

Army Form C. 2118.

Place	Date	Hour	Summary of Events and Information	Remarks and references to Appendices
COUIN.	1/6/18		Rifle 2 P.A. No. 201657 Sgt NAYLOR. E. Wounded to 2g. B. E.E.S. on 24/4/18 & This 305 Sr MITER J Wounded to E.E.S. on 20/4/18 & took church & through. Leader gun.	[sig]
Do.	2/6/18		Rifle 2 P.A. Leader gun.	[sig]
Do.	3/6/18		Rifle 2 P.A. Leader gun.	[sig]
Do.	4/6/18		Rifle 2 P.A. I.M.D. Luth., No. 29. died. Leader gun.	[sig]
Do.	5/6/18		Rifle 2 P.A. Rgr. W. BROWNE. E.F. (Attached to 6g) Proceeded to CALAIS (AUDRUICQ) R.E. G. 2f Army 10/45 dated 29/4/18) Leader I.R.C.	[sig]
Do.	6/6/18		Rifle 2 P.A. No. 74334 LAC DENNY. B.M. 167430 Ist. ACK FAIRBROTHER. W.T. No. 70495 Sr BRADBURY. W.T. No. 70425 Dr. BUTLER. E.H. No. 70429 Sr. FOSTER reinforced from AK 10/15 dated on 28/4/18. No. 75 ScM Q.M. MAYER. P. 0333 SMA QM. MAYER. P. [Continued.]	

WAR DIARY
or
INTELLIGENCE SUMMARY.
(Erase heading not required.)

Army Form C. 2118.

No. 1 COMPANY,
41st
DIVISIONAL TRAIN.

Place	Date	Hour	Summary of Events and Information	Remarks and references to Appendices
ROUEN	6/5/18	Continued	Strength 16 O.C.S. 23/4/18 A/S/Sgt W. PARKES A No 18728 O.R. WATEFORD J No 20523 Ofc POULTER E (252 Empire R?) Sent to NA unfit 29/4/18. No 16567 SAMSON W.S (274 Empire R?) Received Ron 286 Empire R to Ra 28/4/18. No. 9816 TOTE Closed up P.C.S.A. 1/5/18 No 355645 Pte THATCHER J & No 400180 Pte BAIRD A joined from 287 Employment Coy SyR. W.S. & one man's ? MS a 30/4/18 wounded & struck off strength gone	[signature]
	7/5/18		Return of work. Lands stables	[signature]
	8/5/18		Return of work No 31699 Pte COLEMAN returned to duty w/days furlough to Paris Rue	[signature]
	9/5/18		Reply to letter. No duties longer attached 15 OR 1 mule infected sudden fever	[signature]

Army Form C. 2118.

No. 1 COMPANY,
41st
DIVISIONAL TRAIN.
Date...........

WAR DIARY
or
INTELLIGENCE SUMMARY.
(Erase heading not required.)

Instructions regarding War Diaries and Intelligence Summaries are contained in F. S. Regs., Part II. and the Staff Manual respectively. Title pages will be prepared in manuscript.

Place	Date	Hour	Summary of Events and Information	Remarks and references to Appendices
COLIN.	10/5/16		Right of Draft. Walsh. Jones	B.W.
Do.	11/5/16		Right of Draft. No. 400509 Pte. Ripley G. (3rd Emp. Bn.) Transferred to No. 2 Coy. Walsh. Jones	T.B.W.
Do.	12/5/16		Right of Draft. No. 30623 S/Sgt Dolan A. (3rd Emp. Bn.) Transferred to 24/11/15 C.A.S.C. Coy received orders to proceed to follow in Breyfe H.D. overnight	B.A.J.
Do.	13/5/16		Right of Draft. Broken Fog. N.C.	B.W.
Do.	14/5/16		No cycle. Coy. Employed at quarters to R.M. No. 130570 Pte. HANDS D. Grand Eqp. 25rd Emp. Coy. & No. 10/1373 S/C. WASON A. Struck from A.S.C. Const. Roll. Shutter 70/13/16 June	B.W.

WAR DIARY or **INTELLIGENCE SUMMARY.**
(Erase heading not required.)

Army Form C. 2118.

Place	Date	Hour	Summary of Events and Information	Remarks and references to Appendices
LA LOUVIE CHATEAU	15/9/17		3rd Runway at WAAYENBURG at 10 A.M. & Watch to Camp for LOUVIE Chateau. Arrived W.B. 2-30 P.M. No 75 Games Gp. WATSOUA. Nos. Ref. J 109 B.A. Battn line.	JP
LEICESTER CAMP	16/9/17		Cas. Order to LEICESTER Camp. Arrived 8 P.M. INTERNATIONAL CORNER to PESELHOEK BA... Life of LOUVIE DAM 3 at Our Camping G.P.N. No 7169 D FRANKS 3 Rest high Enemy bombing & Arty obser. Sq. S.A.I.S.N.R. first 2nd Dismounted & G.H.Q. sighting & wounded on English G/75 6 bombing 10 Enemy Aeroplane.	JP
Do	17/9/17 →		Order B.P.N. No "4-449/65" Regt. CARR. F.A. 5/2/2 G16 ECS 4/14/14 9 Stuck if - all times to Stud arrived from Europe at night to Lords in Recen. 6 Planes. Lt. Enemy bombing Batter fire 9 Rpt.	JP
Between Peselhoek & Leicester Camp	18/9/17		Regt. and to Report to Corps to Peselhoek on N.W. Side of PESELHOEK — WOESTEN Road left lot 125 Brother Gun O.K.E.	JP

WAR DIARY
or
INTELLIGENCE SUMMARY.
(Erase heading not required.)

Army Form C. 2118.

Place	Date	Hour	Summary of Events and Information	Remarks and references to Appendices
Woods nr PESELHOEK-WOESTEN Rd.	19/5/16		Relief B Coy. 6th R. Lanc. (Less C) to sig nr Coy HQ Rain.	
Do.	20/5/16	7 A.M.	Relieve H.A.M. Anzyi Rqn fair & diving night at Sig. Sch hr. - G.H.Q. Reserve	
Do.	21/5/16		Reld. HAM Batln Hre	
Do.	22/5/16	1 A.M.	Reld. HAM 2nd Q. Yorks to R [illeg] Vanheule Farm R Oliver & Ritchie wounded to 25 FA Rich Sqn 2 No. 93.109. Sgt. Frank J sickened to 25 FA Pk [illeg] 1 Rich Sqn 2	
Do.	23/5/16		Reld. HAM. Work Rive	
Do.	24/5/16		Reld. HAM 20 & 2/5 A&C. handed to rgmt Sgt Hoe & OC Lost Sgt Gahl Lepre & with ren 2 Buff Sig & gave to 25 FA Hosprl sgn Cpl. Watson gained F/A 1 Sqt. G2 Faribrother WT. discharged from Hosprl sgn. 2 Lt. W.R.P.	

Army Form C. 2118.

No. 1. COMPANY,
41ST
DIVISIONAL TRAIN.

WAR DIARY
or
INTELLIGENCE SUMMARY.
(Erase heading not required.)

Instructions regarding War Diaries and Intelligence Summaries are contained in F. S. Regs., Part II. and the Staff Manual respectively. Title pages will be prepared in manuscript.

Place	Date	Hour	Summary of Events and Information	Remarks and references to Appendices
ISDEGEM / RESELHOEK ROAD	21/9/18		Officer I/C A.M. I.H.9. admitted 52nd AVS (wounded) W/R fire	
	24/9/18		Officer I/C A.M. No 7,390 Spr. RUSSELL admitted 103rd F.A. with R.S. Fire	
	25/9/18			

WAR DIARY
or
INTELLIGENCE SUMMARY
(Erase heading not required.)

Army Form C. 2118.

Place	Date	Hour	Summary of Events and Information	Remarks and references to Appendices
WOODCOTE FARM PASSCHENDAELE	19/5/18	11 A.M.	Relief. Weather fine.	
Do.	29/5/18	11 A.M.	Relief. 11 A.M. No.74 & No.75 O.P. Relieved by Lieut. FAIRBROTHER W.T. & No.7354 Dvr. GORDON L. of 135 F.A. Relieved — Sergt. 13295 F.A. Weather fine.	
Do.	30/5/18	11 A.M.	Relief. Weather fine.	
Do.	31/5/18	11 A.M.	Relief. 11 A.M. No.74328 Dr. WILSON J.F. attached 135 F.A. & No.105 MacKENZIE G.D. A.V.S. Relieved. Weather fine.	

O.C. No.1 Co. 41st Divisional Train

WAR DIARY
or
INTELLIGENCE SUMMARY.
(Erase heading not required.)

Army Form C. 2118.

NO. 1 COMPANY.
41ST DIVISIONAL TRAIN.

Place	Date	Hour	Summary of Events and Information	Remarks and references to Appendices
BOIS W.D. POPERINGE - EYKHOEK RD.	1/6/18		Refile 11 A.M. Shelter gone.	By
Do.	2/6/18		Refile 11 A.M. No 77019 Dr. Gee FARBROTHER W.S. discharged Gen. 12/5 Ayte & Sykes injd by M. G. Fire in Picking Gnr. G. Hunt on duck.	By
Do.	3/6/18		Refile 11 A.M. No 7134 Dr. HIGDON L.E. discharged to E.S.A. No. 72379 Dr. JOHNSON J.F. Wounded to C.C.S. ?.3/5/18. Gnr on duty. Pte. succeeded 3/5/18 Officer on duty	By
Do.	4/6/18		Refile 11 A.M. Shelter gone.	By
Do.	5/6/18		Refile 11 A.M. No. 77/560 Dr: ASHW R. admitted to LoC/c 1 A Duty. 123/106 Rfld Dr. C. Bruno Duty 1H S ?? d 27/5/15? Gnr on Shelter one	By

WAR DIARY
INTELLIGENCE SUMMARY
(Erase heading not required.)

Army Form C. 2118.

NO. 1 COMPANY,
41ST
DIVISIONAL TRAIN.

Place	Date	Hour	Summary of Events and Information	Remarks and references to Appendices
BAMBECQUE Area.	1/6/18		Company moved to BAMBECQUE area 5-6.30 A.M. Refilled Water Carts 9.30 P.M. Batten fine.	13B
BOLLEZEELE Area.	2/6/18		March returned to BOLLEZEELE area. Pans 3-10 A.M. Refilled w/ Carts 1 P.M. Weather fine.	12B
RUMINGHEM Area	3/6/18		March returned to RUMINGHEM area. Pans 5-6.30 A.M. Refilled W/ Carts 1 P.M. arrived S.O.T. 9 P.M. Weather fine. Baggage of Canny [?]	14B
Do.	4/6/18		Refill to Coy from 3rd & 4th D.R. Capt. FULLER I. & Major D. HUTCHINSON G.S.O. N.G.S.L. attd. for Instruction. Capt. Knight M.B. Lieut. Relted in S/D High Church H Dumford. Weather fine	7B
Do.	5/6/18		Refill W/ Cuts of 5th Inf. Bn. Weather fine	13B

WAR DIARY

INTELLIGENCE SUMMARY.

(Erase heading not required.)

No. 1 COMPANY,
41st DIVISIONAL TRAIN.

Army Form C. 2118.

Place	Date	Hour	Summary of Events and Information	Remarks and references to Appendices
RUMINGHEM area	11/9/16		No. 74540 Dr. ASH W.R. discharged from hospital. Transferred to Machine Gun Corps. Duty reported Butter fire.	SR
Do.	14/9/16		Supply drawn by Motor Transport to WATTEN. Discharged 10-15 AM No. T3573 Dr. BEEVERS F. admitted to 122 F.A. Butter fire.	SR
Do.	15/9/16		Returned to duty 12.15 AM No. T4640 Dr EASY M. wounded 6PM E.C.S. No. T4640 Dr. ASH W.R. admitted to 122 F.A. Butter fire.	SR
Do.	14/9/16		Returned to duty 12.15 PM from No. T4690 Dr. PATTISON H. admitted 10/9/16 to 128 F.A. No. T4647 Dr. EASY M. reported from E.C.S. & taken on strength. Butter fire.	SR
Do.	15/9/16		Returned to duty No. T3573 Dr. BEEVERS F. discharged from 128 F.A. Butter fire.	SR

WAR DIARY
INTELLIGENCE SUMMARY

Army Form C. 2118.

No. 1 COMPANY,
41st DIVISIONAL TRAIN.

Place	Date	Hour	Summary of Events and Information	Remarks and references to Appendices
RUNINGHEM	16/6/16		Railed to hospital No: 30733 Pte WASON A. Transferred to base (HAVRE) through to England on Cyto attached. Funeral No 30159 Pte ANDERSON E Transferred to Q.M. & No: 30558 Pte JOHNSON E. Transferred from Old 2nd Transferred from Cyto. Bullet fire	
Do.	17/6/16		Railhead as usual. Bullet fire.	
Do.	18/6/16		Ringing of hospital No: 14099 Dr. PATTISON H. Sicknessfield No: SS & ES also of Sgt/Maj SheyR. No: 15030 Dr. ASH.W.R. discharged from 183rd F.A. 12850 Bullet fine	
Do.	19/6/16		Railhead as usual. Bullet Shelling.	
Do.	20/6/16		Railhead as usual. Bullet fire.	
Do.	21/6/16		Railhead as usual. Bullet fire. No: 17/5A EMSY attached W.S.O. Vice Major MacKay proceeding to leave.	

Army Form C. 2118.

NO. 1 COMPANY,
41st
DIVISIONAL TRAIN.

WAR DIARY
or
INTELLIGENCE SUMMARY.
(Erase heading not required.)

Instructions regarding War Diaries and Intelligence Summaries are contained in F. S. Regs., Part II. and the Staff Manual respectively. Title pages will be prepared in manuscript.

Place	Date	Hour	Summary of Events and Information	Remarks and references to Appendices
RUMINGHEM WR.	22/5/16		Railhead W Wizernes. Weather fine	[A]
Do.	23/5/16		Railhead Wizernes. Recd. No. T4/705 Dr. ANDREWS, G.F. admitted to 122nd F.A. Weather fine	[B]
Do.	24/5/16		Railhead Wizernes. Recd. No. SH/9105/104 Pte HALLIDAY W.H. posted from 4th Reserve Regt & Pte Story R.W. from 5 HQ's. Pte Gilbert & Pte Deerwood from RHQ in G & John. B. Bengla. Weather Showery	[C]
Do.	25/5/16		Railhead Wizernes. Company marched out 20 A.M. & ZEGGERS CAPPEL. Supply Lorry's Parked & Supply arrived 8 my rifles & delivered. Arrived at 11.30 at S/Sgt VINALL A.H.D. 2 Lieutg. No. 1184 G.S. 1954 Dy No. F. 104209 transferred to Aff.I. Depot at ABBEVILLE as Supply No substitutes (to Strength Weather fine	[D]

WAR DIARY
INTELLIGENCE SUMMARY

Army Form C. 2118.

No. 1 COMPANY,
41st DIVISIONAL TRAIN.

Place	Date	Hour	Summary of Events and Information	Remarks and references to Appendices
STEENVOORDE AREA	26/5/16		Company arrived in camp in STEENVOORDE area. Supplies delivered by M.T. to A.S.C. cars from 2.20 P.M. Weather fine.	
do.	27/5/16		Rifle in camp from M.T. (?) Weather fine.	
do.	28/5/16		Rifle at 9 a.m. & 3 P.M. Weather stormy.	
do.	29/5/16		Quartermaster returned from leave, arrived at STEENVOORDE. Arrived 9.30 P.M. (?) in camp 10 P.M. Weather fine.	
do.	30/5/16		Received at 10.30 (?) one day's half ordinary supplied to camp by detached units. Return (?) to Q.M.H. Supplies (?)	

O.C. No. 1 Company,
41st Div. Train.

Army Form C. 2118.

NO. 1 COMPANY,
41ST DIVISIONAL TRAIN.

No. ....
Date ....

WAR DIARY
or
INTELLIGENCE SUMMARY.
(Erase heading not required.)

Instructions regarding War Diaries and Intelligence Summaries are contained in F. S. Regs., Part II. and the Staff Manual respectively. Title pages will be prepared in manuscript.

Place	Date	Hour	Summary of Events and Information	Remarks and references to Appendices
STEENVOORDE	1/7/16		Supply delivered at 6:30 A.M. to Lughunghur 2nd Inf. Supplies to Greenspitt Camp from Steenvoorde Mystery 10:15 A.M. & refilled at Camp large Supply issued. Number 75's Staff lee MAHER P. Supplied from P.S.E. Coys 1 T.S. HAVRE 93rd later on Strength. Shelter Pve.	19 A
WATON FRANCE FARM				
Do.	2/7/16		Rushed ex B 1st Inf. Refld 2.30 P.M. 1 mule loss Rfld is 52nd & 1 S.B. Warden (Davidson Sergt.) Co. T.3.R. CASEY M.T. 4-7:30 93rd CATTERALL H. Struck off Strgth & later A Strgth. 30-6-16 B when due.	19 R
Do.	3/7/16		Rushed & Refld H & D 2nd Inf. 1 mule loss (mule kicked) (Nos 2 & 40) & 1 H.Q. No.9 Sheranded & Struck off Strgth. Written one.	19 C
Do.	4/7/16		Rushed & Refld 4 of 2nd Ind. 2 A.D. Lives (Nos 125 & 126), damaged & wheeled to No 2 Coys Sheranded & Struck off Strgth. Brake gr.	19 D

T2134. Wt. W708—776. 500000. 4/15. Sir J. C. & S.

WAR DIARY
or
~~INTELLIGENCE SUMMARY~~

(Erase heading not required.)

Army Form C. 2118.

NO. 1 COMPANY.
41ST DIVISIONAL TRAIN.

Instructions regarding War Diaries and Intelligence Summaries are contained in F. S. Regs., Part II. and the Staff Manual respectively. Title pages will be prepared in manuscript.

Place	Date	Hour	Summary of Events and Information	Remarks and references to Appendices
STEENVOORDE area, WATON, FRANCE	5/7/16		Railhead & refill as usual. No. T3 Supplies &c. S/Sgt. Abrahams to No. 4 Coy. No. S/8169 S/Sgt. G. BAWDEN to A.S.C. Base Dep. as Supplier T3 Detachment. Weather fine.	748
Do.	6/7/16		Railhead & refill as usual. Company lines & fields inspected by G.O.C. Weather fine.	748
Do.	7/7/16		Refill & railhead as usual. Weather fine.	748
Do.	8/7/16		Refill & railhead as usual. No. T3/3338 Stable Sgt. MAHER P.K. Sgt.) Weather fine.	748
Do.	9/7/16		Railhead & refill as usual. No. T4/046746 A. HARRISON S/Sgt. Shg. Smith to 1st Sgt. MAIR R. Rmd. Sm. Sgt. Div. Sm. Futter & Shg.Sm. No. T4/046757 Sr. S.S. T. attached 186th F.A. (Sadler & Bmk^{er})	748

WAR DIARY

INTELLIGENCE SUMMARY

(Erase heading not required.)

Army Form C. 2118.

No. 1 COMPANY,
41st DIVISIONAL TRAIN.

Instructions regarding War Diaries and Intelligence Summaries are contained in F. S. Regs., Part II. and the Staff Manual respectively. Title pages will be prepared in manuscript.

Place	Date	Hour	Summary of Events and Information	Remarks and references to Appendices
STEENVOORDE AREA. WATON FRANCE FARM.	10/7/16		Railhead & cattle at Mmal. H.Q. Coys. Nos. 1,2,3 & 62nd A.V.S. Standing by. 5 Lnfycted & in full Annamel Onmarching order Commanding Officer abt 2-30 P.M. Izalen Stormy 15C	ASR
Do	11/7/16		Railhead & cattle at Mmal. H.Q. No. 1,2,3 Inspected & Such M(Gomety) H.Q. No. 3, 5 Billetts to Stable fire & Such It. Walker Stormy 15C	ASR
Do	12/7/16		Railhead & cattle at Mmal. Weather Stormy & 15C.	ASR
Do	13/7/16		Railhead & cattle at Mmal. Weather fine.	ASR
Do	14/7/16		Railhead & cattle at Mmal. Weather 15C	ASR
Do	15/7/16		Railhead & cattle at Mmal. 1 Mule No. 14 Evacuated to s2 M.V.S. & Such It Sloyk Weather Stormy	ASR

No. 1 COMPANY.
41ST DIVISIONAL TRAIN.

Army Form C. 2118.

WAR DIARY
or
INTELLIGENCE SUMMARY.
(Erase heading not required.)

Instructions regarding War Diaries and Intelligence Summaries are contained in F. S. Regs., Part II. and the Staff Manual respectively. Title pages will be prepared in manuscript.

Place	Date	Hour	Summary of Events and Information	Remarks and references to Appendices
STEENVOORDE AREA WATON FRANCE. FARM	16/7/18		Railhead & refill as usual. All detailed Infantry return. Sgt. HALLIDAY. W.H. admitted 138 F.Amb. Sick. Give No.14 14/30/04	
Do.	17/7/18		Railhead & refill as usual. All details return. Mile 1 Triangle No. 669.3 Received from Ordnance & taken on strength. Bowker Gun.	
Do.	18/7/18		Railway & refill as usual. Supply wagon 156 Bde A.F.A. attached Sups & engr. Supply wagon S.A.A. section D.A.C. Green Bn. detached Ple & engr. Supply wagon of M.G. Bn. detached to engr. Lewis gun.	
Do.	19/5/18		Railroad & refill as usual. Lewis Gun.	

WAR DIARY or INTELLIGENCE SUMMARY

Army Form C. 2118.

No. 1 COMPANY, 41ST DIVISIONAL TRAIN.

Place	Date	Hour	Summary of Events and Information	Remarks and references to Appendices
STEENVOORDE AREA WATON FRAME FARM.	20/5/18		Railhead & refill as usual. No. T4/08833 Sgt: LOW.E. joined from ABS. Rft. Sgt: A. Statham struck off strength. No. 201559 Pte: DIVERION. J (ASC Employed Base) Evacuated to S.S. 14.F. & Struck off Strength.	75R
Do.	21/5/18		Railhead & refill as usual.	75R
Do.	22/5/18		Railhead & refill as usual. No. T4/065143 Dr: ANDREWS.G.F. Evacuated to England on 11.5.18 & Struck off Strength.	75R
Do.	23/5/18		Railhead & refill as usual.	75R
Do.	24/5/18		Railhead & refill as usual. No. 26050 Pte: DAWSON.W. returned to duty W.E.F. 9.5.18. Employed as A.1.B.S. wef. & Struck off Strength.	75R

WAR DIARY
or
~~INTELLIGENCE SUMMARY~~

(Erase heading not required.)

Army Form C. 2118.

No. 1 COMPANY,
41st
DIVISIONAL TRAIN.

No. ....
Date ....

Place	Date	Hour	Summary of Events and Information	Remarks and references to Appendices
STEENVOORDE Area. NrTON FRANCE	24/7/18	Parade	Railed & refill of Intral. Pte Johnny Ainsworth joined from ATS Aust. Sgt Lilly. Shay.R. No.74573 Sheila G.E. Luff. S.P. No.765445 Dr. McShane.M. No.765445 Dr. Martindill.F.W. No.785544 Dr. Marsden.J. No.763726 Pte. Hems.R. No.394409 Dvr. McCann.N.J. & No.757726 138 F.A. No. 54101 Sgt. Halliday.W.A. rejoined from Rouen fire.	
Do.	26/7/18		Railed & refill of Intral. S.H.D. Lves received for Rimmond BSM W.M & Peter & Shay.R.	
Do.	27/7/18		Railed & refill of Intral. Peake 226.	
Do.	28/7/18		Railed & refill of Intral. No.645886 Pte. Griffiths.E.R. transferred from 20th Div Train. No.T5 Havin C/E Crockford F.W. admitted to Hospital. Isolation fire	

WAR DIARY
or
INTELLIGENCE SUMMARY.
(Erase heading not required.)

Army Form C. 2118.

Place	Date	Hour	Summary of Events and Information	Remarks and references to Appendices
STEENVOORDE AREA. WATON FRANCE FARM.	29/7/15		Railhead & refile as usual.	
Do.	30/7/15		Railhead & refile as usual. Hand in horses No. 01688 Dr. SEED J. reported sick. Isolation line.	
Do.	31/7/15		Railhead & refile as usual.	

R. Parker Major ASC

WAR DIARY or INTELLIGENCE SUMMARY

Army Form C. 2118.

No. 1 COMPANY,
41st DIVISIONAL TRAIN.

Place	Date	Hour	Summary of Events and Information	Remarks and references to Appendices
STEENVOORDE AREA. NORD FRANCE	1/8/16		Railhead & refill as usual. A.S.C. personnel & vehicles attached from 150th Inf. Bde. A.F.A. rejoined this Unit on 31st July. Weather fine.	
Do	2/8/16		Railhead & refill as usual. All lugage drawn to amm. Pk. cham. from sundry Company Bakers. Weather fine.	
Do	3/8/16		Railhead & refill as usual. No. 78 Driver Pte. W. ROCKFORD, E.W. rejoined from hospital. No. S.S.M. DUGGAN, H.J. attached to 124 Infantry Bde. on 31st ulto. Originally evacuated for Railway Employment.	
Do	4/8/16		Railhead & refill as usual. No. T4030 Driver Pte. FARBROTHER, W.T. transferred to A.S.C. Local Depot at Boulogne K Establishment. Weather fine.	

WAR DIARY
or
INTELLIGENCE SUMMARY.
(Erase heading not required.)

Army Form C. 2118.

NO. 1 COMPANY,
41st
DIVISIONAL TRAIN.
No. ....
Date. ....

Instructions regarding War Diaries and Intelligence Summaries are contained in F.S. Regs., Part II. and the Staff Manual respectively. Title pages will be prepared in manuscript.

Place	Date	Hour	Summary of Events and Information	Remarks and references to Appendices
STEENVOORDE AREA NORD FRANCE FARM.	5/8/18		Refill & railhead & Iond. No.7 & 8 SP PARNELL W. Warn Lab to N.Z. 5/Chesh Lgths on 27/6/18 + 8 trans. of F.Coy.R. No 770 Pte HEMS R.A. Cyclists 15 No. 18 Evn to Evn 65 Inf B Denothes Station.	
Do.	6/8/18		Railhead & refill as Usual. Rather Showery	
Do.	7/8/18		Railhead + as usual as Usual. Rather Fine.	
Do.	8/8/18		Railhead + refill as Usual. Rather Fine.	
Do.	9/8/18		Railhead + refill as Usual. 1 Rider No. 18 returned to S.B.D M.Y.S. Rather Fine.	
Do.	10/8/18		Railhead + refill as Usual. Rather Fine. Entrained to Oost Cleer	

T2134. Wt. W708-776. 500000. 4/16. Sir J.C. & S.

WAR DIARY
or
INTELLIGENCE SUMMARY
(Erase heading not required.)

Army Form C. 2118.

[Stamp: . . COMPANY, 41st DIVISIONAL TRAIN.]

Place	Date	Hour	Summary of Events and Information	Remarks and references to Appendices
STEENVOORDE AREA.				
WATOU RANGE FARM			The undermentioned O.R's to base Stowd from A.S.C. Ants Depot.	
Continued from last Sheet	10/8/18		No. T/31210 Dr. POW. W. No. T/41123 Dr. POTTER. E.M.	
			" T/31367 " PARKER. J. " T/32404 " PURCHASE. A.E.	
			" T/35695 " PRIEST. G. " T/38695 " POWELL. V.B.	
			" T/39224 " PAGE. E. " T/39260 " QUINN. P.	
			" T/41349 " PRICE. J. " T/39380 " ROSS. G.A.	
	11/8/18		Railhead & 9th Bn. Stand. No. T/41030 Dr. FRASER. I. admitted to 138th Field Ambulance. Sick Furl.	
Do.	12/8/18		The undermentioned O.R's were transferred to A.S.C. Ants Depôt.	
			HAKE 2. Ionite to Infantry.	
			No. T/3664 Dr. BOOTHMAN C.H. No. T/28712 Dr. HARPER. T. No. M/37379 Dr. MAYERS. J.	
			" T/43294 " CAMDEN G.W. " T/31064 " HIGDON. L.G. " M/2203 " SPARKS. R.A.	
			" T/36655 " DAVIES. R.J. " T/31464 " JEANS. H.G.	
			" T/31515 " FARR. W. " T/36491 " JOY. H.A.	
				Continued on next Sheet.

WAR DIARY
or
INTELLIGENCE SUMMARY.
(Erase heading not required.)

Army Form C. 2118.

No. 1 COMPANY,
41ST
DIVISIONAL TRAIN.

Place	Date	Hour	Summary of Events and Information	Remarks and references to Appendices
STEENVOORDE AREA.				
Wagon Range Farm Arrived from Outtersteene	12/6/16		Railhead & refill of bread. No. 74 T/43760 Pte FRASER D. evacuated 15 Casualty Clearing Stn. 115 M.T. 2091/60 struck off strength. No. 1 Order No.3 12. Evacuated from 53 M.F.S. by H.S. "St Sr---" to 16 Ambulance interchangeable. Own horsed Coy. 286 Employment Coy. M.T.C.A.S.C 4 Horses. No.159572 S/S ILETT A. M/93287, Pte SWEENEY. T. taken sick.	782
Do.	13/8/16		Railhead & refill of bread No. 74. T/43762 Sgt HINES J. admitted 15 C.C.S. 238 A.A.D. 123 kill. taken sick.	782
Do.	14/8/16		Railhead & refill of bread. No. 74. T/43762 Sgt HINES J. evacuated 15 Cavalry C.C.S on 15" 238 A.A.D. struck off strength. W.O. 149375 Cpl SCARLETT Fork No. 15137 Aligtroke struck off. W.O. 149375 Cpl SCARLETT W. W. J. attached for ration & quarters No.174 T/72360 Dr. PLOWDEN VAN Ringtyne fire do. S.A.P. taken sick.	782
Do.	15/6/16		Railhead & refill of bread. taken sick.	782

Army Form C. 2118.

WAR DIARY
or
INTELLIGENCE SUMMARY.
(Erase heading not required.)

Instructions regarding War Diaries and Intelligence Summaries are contained in F. S. Regs., Part II. and the Staff Manual respectively. Title pages will be prepared in manuscript.

No. 1 COMPANY.
41st
DIVISIONAL TRAIN.
No....................
Date..................

Place	Date	Hour	Summary of Events and Information	Remarks and references to Appendices
STEENVOORDE AREA WALON FRANCE FARM	15/9/16		Railhead & refill as usual. Weather fine.	1/9/16
Do.	16/9/16		Railhead & refill as usual. Remaining for divl. train. 6.H.S. lorries received from Butler. Fine and...	16/9
Do.	17/9/16		Railhead & refill as usual. 2.H.S. lorries received from Reynolds in B. Butler to Reynolds. The remaining 4 Butler to H.S. Engines.	17/9
Do.	18/9/16		Railhead & refill as usual. Weather fine.	18/9
Do.	19/9/16		Railhead & refill as usual. 1 Double (W.D.) admitted to 52 W.S. Wounded. 1 Officers Vehicles inspected in afternoon by D.S. & T. Weather fine.	19/9
Do.	20/9/16		Railhead & refill as usual. 1 Double (W.D.) struck off strength. Weather fine. Very hot.	20/9

T2134. Wt. W708—776. 500000. 4/15. Sir J. C. & S.

WAR DIARY
INTELLIGENCE SUMMARY

Army Form C. 2118

NO. 1 COMPANY,
41ST DIVISIONAL TRAIN.

Place	Date	Hour	Summary of Events and Information	Remarks and references to Appendices
STEENVOORDE AREA WATON FRANCE FARM	22/8/18		Railhead & refill as usual. Pte L.D. Oriole drawn from Reinfts.	B.
Do	23/8/18		Railhead & refill as usual. Draft received of 28 O.Rs.+ 1 S.Sgt. 12 Infantry & 16 A.S.C. Strength of Strength — 2 S.Sgts, 1 Stf Sgt, No T 30/; Sgts L.D.R. MER F Christie 1335 A.A. for No: 9 Sg on 25 Infgr.	B.
Do	24/8/18		Railhead & refill as usual. Pte No.150 Bagnall Hugh 52 to T.B.D. Struck off Strength. Weather fine.	B.
Do	25/8/18		Railhead & refill as usual. Weather fine.	B.
Do	26/8/18		Railhead & refill as usual. No 202064 Pte Drake T. attacked from 285 Employment Coy to Asher B.H.	B.
Do	27/8/18		Railhead & refill as usual. No:151892 Pte Ileit H returned to 285 Employment Coy Asher B.H.	B.

Army Form C. 2118.

No. 1 COMPANY.
41st DIVISIONAL TRAIN.
No. ....
Date. ....

WAR DIARY
or
INTELLIGENCE SUMMARY.
(Erase heading not required.)

Instructions regarding War Diaries and Intelligence Summaries are contained in F. S. Regs., Part II. and the Staff Manual respectively. Title pages will be prepared in manuscript.

Place	Date	Hour	Summary of Events and Information	Remarks and references to Appendices
STEENVOORDE AREA. WATON FRANCE FARM.	28/8/18		Railhead & refill as usual. Butter issued.	
Do.	29/8/18		Railhead & refill as usual. No 73. & 74. S/Sgt: HARWOOD W.J. Kirkland S.S.E. Divisional Supply Column Struck off Strength & Posted to 84th Divisional Train. Butter & New Zealand Frozen Mutton issued for Supplies.	(MS.B.)
Do.	30/8/18		Refill Column as usual. No. 7. & 68. T.S.M. DUGGAN M.J. signed over from 235 Employment Coy (Labour) No: 98248 for Employment Commission. Butter issued.	
Do.	31/8/18		Supply Column from STEENVOORDE to WATOU FRANCE FARM. 10:30 A.M. Capt. E.M.WOOD D.S.A. Calling attached 102 F.A. to Withdraw to Base. Butter issued.	

O.C. 1 Coy. 41st Div: Trn.

Army Form C. 2118.

WAR DIARY
or
INTELLIGENCE SUMMARY.
(Erase heading not required.)

Halloy H.S. Det. Amm

Place	Date	Hour	Summary of Events and Information	Remarks and references to Appendices
STEENVOORDE AREA.				
WATON FRANCE FARM	12/9/15		Relief Sup. A.S.C. at ABEELE arrived 2.30 P.M. Company moved to Camp IV ABEELE water fine	AM
New ABEELE	2/9/15		Company moved to Camp E ABEELE or ABEELE — RENINGHELST Road. Rifles in the Camp for M.T. at 2 P.M. water fine	AR
ABEELE — RENINGHELST Road.	3/9/15		Company moved. Moving over ABEELE machine occupied in 1st Sups. Rifles for M.T. in Camp. Rifle testing water fine	11&P
New ABEELE	4/9/15		Relief Sup. M.T. & Aeroplane 9 P.M. Company E. M. WOOD assigned from to 2 Field Ambulance water fine	P.S.
Do.	5/9/15		Relief 2 A.15 mt. 2 Rolls + 1 Amb. received from Reinforcements water fine	AP.

T2134. Wt. W708—776. 500000. 4/15. Sir J. C. & S.

WAR DIARY
or
~~INTELLIGENCE SUMMARY.~~
(Erase heading not required.)

Army Form C. 2118.

Place	Date	Hour	Summary of Events and Information	Remarks and references to Appendices
Near ABEELE	6/9/16		Battalion in 15 A.F.A. Brigade formed on Aerodrome at 2 P.M. Route march	
Do.	7/9/16		Company Drills B Coy A ABEELE POPERINGHE Road. S.W. of POPERINGE. Rest of Battalion from the WIPPENHOEK Railhead to ABEELE Rifle Open Range at 1 P.M. 50 yds of S.M.L.E. RIFLE & Bayonet 15 yds Australian E.I.S. or 80 lists + Punch off Butts. Coy	
Near POPERINGE	8/9/16	8.45 A.M.	Railhead WIPPENHOEK Supplies drawn by Motor Transport. Weather Stormy to B.n. Left to A.Q.n.	
Do.	9/9/16		Railhead + supply as AD inds Butler B.C.	
Do.	10/9/16		Railhead + supplies as Issued. Buffs Coy discount have required Weather Showery Company	

WAR DIARY
or
INTELLIGENCE SUMMARY.
(Erase heading not required.)

Army Form C. 2118.

Motor M.T. Coy. Names

Place	Date	Hour	Summary of Events and Information	Remarks and references to Appendices
Nr. POPERINGHE	11/9/18		Railhead 11 A.M. Refile 1 P.M. Weather Showery	BR
Do.	12/9/18		Railhead 11 A.M. Refile 1 P.M. Weather wet.	Fine
- Do -	13/9/18		Railhead 11 A.M. Refile 1 P.M. Weather wet.	Fine
- Do -	14/9/18		- Do - - Do -	Fine
- Do -	15/9/18		Railhead 11 A.M. Refile 1 P.M. Weather fine. No 7/14568 T.S.S.M. Duggan H.J. proceeded to England for admission to Cadet School. No 201663 D. Manuel J. (288 Employment Coy) admitted to hospital	Fine
- Do -	16/9/18		Railhead 11 A.M. Refile 1 P.M. No 7/370595 D. Priest G. transferred to A.S.C. Base Depot. HAVRE & struck off. No 201693 Pte. Manuel J. discharged from 138 F.A. Weather fine.	Fine

Army Form C. 2118.

WAR DIARY
or
INTELLIGENCE SUMMARY.
(Erase heading not required.)

Instructions regarding War Diaries and Intelligence Summaries are contained in F. S. Regs., Part II. and the Staff Manual respectively. Title pages will be prepared in manuscript.

Place	Date	Hour	Summary of Events and Information	Remarks and references to Appendices
Near POPERINGE	17/9/18		Reached 10.45 A.M. Refill 1 P.M. 1 H.D. Horse No 58 admitted to 52 M.V.S. No 74/042418 D. Withers Transferred from T.H.Q. & No T4/242660 D. Plowden V. Transferred to T.H.Q. Weather fine	Fine
	18.9.18		Reached 10.45 A.M. Refill 1 P.M. No T/302600 D. Cooper E. Transferred to 30" Div Train. The supply waggons of 11" Bde R.F.A. rejoined their Bde. a Ceased to be attached to us. Weather fine	Fine
	19.9.18		Reached 10.45 A.M. The Coy moved to a Camp on the ABEELE - RENINGHELST Rd at Shet 27 L34 C.4.6. Refilled in new camp at 2 p.m. Weather fine	Fine
Shet 27 L34 C.4.6 26.9.18 ABEELE - RENINGHELST ROAD			No Supplies were drawn from Railhead today. 1 H.D. Horse No 58 was admitted to 52 M.V.S. & evacuated & struck off strength 1 H.D. Horse transferred from No 3 Coy taken on the strength Weather fine	Fine

T2134. Wt. W708—776. 500000. 4/16. Sir J. C. & S.

WAR DIARY
or
INTELLIGENCE SUMMARY.
(Erase heading not required.)

Army Form C. 2118.

No 1 Coy H.Q. O.C. Maj. Nau

Place	Date	Hour	Summary of Events and Information	Remarks and references to Appendices
Sheet 27 L34 C 4 6	21/9/18		Railhead 10.45 am. Refill at 12 midday. Weather fine	Fries
	22/9/18		— Do — — Do —	Fries
	23/9/18	10.15 Am.	Railhead 10.15 Am. No S/SR 1152 Pte Pickles, J. admitted to 104" F.A.	Fries
	24/9/18		Railhead 10.15 Am. Refill at 12 midday. Weather fine — Do — 4 divers were sent to units.	Fries
	25/9/18			Fries
	26/9/18	10.15 Am.	Railhead 10.15 Am. Refill at 12 midday. No S/SR 1152 Pte Pickles, J. was evacuated to 62" C.C.S. on 23". Unit struck off strength. Weather fine.	Fries

WAR DIARY
INTELLIGENCE SUMMARY

Army Form C. 2118.

No 1 Cov H. 1 @ Pwl Haw

Place	Date	Hour	Summary of Events and Information	Remarks and references to Appendices
Sheet 27 43b C41 ABEELE	27/9/18		Railhead at 10.16 P.M. Repts at midday 1 HD horse No 27 admitted to 52nd M.V.S. Weather fine.	Pmw
RENINGHELST Rd.	28/9/18		Railhead & refilling of A 235 Inf. Coy arrived to BRAND HOEK at 7 P.M. Weather fine. J.K.D. No 37 Iv. R. W. Staff.	
BRANDHOEK	29/9/18	10AM	Refille from lorries in BRANDHOEK. 1 Am. No 201655 Sgt BUCKLEY. N. attached from D.a.C. Employment Coy 2 Inspected & Evgnd to England to R.A.F. Cadet School. Isstr Starvey in afternoon.	
Do	30/9/18		Refille from lorries of A 29 B at 10AM. Iss Rw L.S.R.	

OC No1 Company H.T. D Pwl Haw

WAR DIARY
~~INTELLIGENCE SUMMARY~~
(Erase heading not required.)

Army Form C. 2118.

No. 1 COMPANY, 41st DIVISIONAL TRAIN.

Place	Date	Hour	Summary of Events and Information	Remarks and references to Appendices
BRANDHOEK.	1/10/18.		Refilled Sup. Am. T. Oeor Euds. D.A.M. No. 74/85/99.6. D2: DICKENS A.E. German arty heavy attack (Gas) honoring on A.S.C. D.A.Os. left. Aerop. field on 62 & E.E.S. Shirts I.P.C. & P.O. Strictly fine. Enemy farm arrived & struck tt. adjoining VOORMEZEELE. I.H.Q. Tube, No.131 Coomte to Ploomties wounded & struck tt.	Post.
VOORMEZEELE	2/10/18.		Refile from M.T. At A YPRES Rod. D.A.M. 1. G.S. Wagn Lost in forward Area & Struck tt. Weather showery.	Post.
	3/10/18.		Refile from M.T. DAM at CAFÉ BELGE — YPRES Rod. Weather fine.	Post.
	4/10/18.		Refile on 2nd Inf. Bde. Grms arr tt S line at BELGIAN BATTERY CORNER. Weather showery.	Post.
BELGIAN BATTERY CORNER.	5/10/18.		Refile on Same rod & on 2nd Inf. Bde Grarer to YPRES. Weather showery.	Post.
	6/10/18.		Refile on 5 Inf. Bde. Weather fine.	Post.

WAR DIARY
or
~~INTELLIGENCE SUMMARY.~~
(Erase heading not required.)

Army Form C. 2118.

No. 1 COMPANY
41st DIVISIONAL TRAIN.

Place	Date	Hour	Summary of Events and Information	Remarks and references to Appendices
BELGIAN BATTERY CORNER	7/10/17		Relieved by a Bt Inf. No: Off: Lockhead J.P. (285 Sof ling rd Rd) Admitted 18D F.A. Brother gunner.	[sig]
Do	8/10/17		Refill as usual. Brother fire.	[sig]
Do	9/10/17		Refill as usual. Brother fire.	[sig]
Do	10/10/17		Refill as usual. Brother fire.	[sig]
Do	11/10/17		Refilling as usual. No. T4466 Dr: Hurren A. admitted 18 F.A. wounded by shell fire. 2 H.D. Kitty admitted 8 2 S.A.V.S. (No: 28+7) wounded by shell fire. 1 H.D. Jenny (No: 189) admitted S.A S.A V.S. & reported (Strick) by 2 Horses (Daisy) + (Struck off) 1 H.D. Luke (No: 127) wounded by shell fire. Brother gun.	[sig]
Do	12/10/17		Refill as usual. Brother W.C.	[sig]

WAR DIARY
or
INTELLIGENCE SUMMARY.
(Erase heading not required.)

Army Form C. 2118.

NO. 1 COMPANY
41st
DIVISIONAL TRAIN.

Place	Date	Hour	Summary of Events and Information	Remarks and references to Appendices
WOODCOTE HOUSE 13/10/18 Sheet 51 20.C.38	13/10/18		Refits as usual. Company ordered to WOODCOTE Hse on Stretford Corner — Lorries & carts. Weather fair.	
Do	14/10/18		Supplies drawn as usual. Remainder of Company arrived at T2015 - R015 at 8.15 AM. Rifle inspection for Coys HQ 8.30 AM. No: 201620 Private LOVELL T.C.G. to England for dental treatment. Coy's carried out gun drill. Examined & fired Coy's C.S.M.G. 27.9.18. No: T/01126 Pte MANNERS, W.R. & No: T/01390 Pte WHITE, F.H. transferred to Company from A.S.C. Base Depot. Weather fine.	
Do	15/10/18		Received & refill as usual. Weather fine.	
DADIZEELE 16/10/18	16/10/18		Company ordered to DADIZEELE 11AM. Billets at Woodcote House. 8AM Supplies delivered. Guns area & a second refill of Rations drawn at MT at 10PM. Every remaining issued on order. No: S4/056656 Sgt GRIFFITHS E.R. admitted 54th F.A. field ambulance. Weather very wet. 1H.9 No: T/S10158 admitted 52nd S.A.V.S. (lame)	

WAR DIARY or INTELLIGENCE SUMMARY

No. 1 COMPANY 41st DIVISIONAL TRAIN

Army Form C. 2118.

Place	Date	Hour	Summary of Events and Information	Remarks and references to Appendices
DADIZEELE	17/10/18		Supplies delivered in lorries by Army MT at the Station Groening	
Do.	18/10/18		Refile of 11th & 12th MT. S.H.D. Lorries Nos 72, 23 & 55 admitted in VS in the Ghent. Butcher line. Wounded & struck off the strength.	
Do.	19/10/18		Refill of 1st & 17th Inf. Butcher line	
Near GULLEGHEM	20/10/18		Company moved to vicinity of GULLEGHEM 14.00. Supplies delivered in lorries; refill at rend. and Art. Butcher Groening	
Near BISSEGHEM	21/10/18		Company moved to BISSEGHEM area at 14.00. Supplies delivered in lorries; refill in new area from MT. 18.30. No. 29932 C.Q.M.S. M.I.L.S.W. admitted No. 5 Field Ambulance Butcher line. Sick	
Do.	22/10/18		Refile from MT. 19.00. SHD received for Remounts Butcher line	

T2134. Wt. W708—776. 500000. 4/15. Sir J. C. & S.

WAR DIARY
or
INTELLIGENCE SUMMARY.
(Erase heading not required.)

Army Form C. 2118.

No. 1 COMPANY,
41ST
DIVISIONAL TRAIN.

Place	Date	Hour	Summary of Events and Information	Remarks and references to Appendices
OSSEGHEM	23/10/18		Refill Sn M.T. 16.30 Nov 74/76. Dr HURREN A. arrived from 188th F.A. No 7458. A/Cpl POSK117 74/76 W joined from A.S.C. Rnft. Depôt Calais. Sne OTF52	748
Do	24/10/18		Refill 15.00 from Sn T. 18 rifles Sne 1H9 (10154) Ordce (N318) Shepherd + Struck off.	748
Do	25/10/18		Reft. No defs. No T3 800092 E.Q.M.S. MILLS W. wounded to C.C.S. + Struck off. Strikes gone.	148
Do.	29/10/18. R.		Refill 07.30 from Sn T. 1 Rifle 9 I.H9 leaving for Renais Sne H.Q. remained in S.O.R. In V.S. (Same) Struck gone.	708
Do.	30/10/18.		Shifted down from LEDEGHEM. arrived by late train for Renaix at 06.20 A.M. Struck gone.	752
Do.	31/10/18		No T's Dr WILKINSON R. syndoned to 823 LINS unit 99th Dr WATTS S.S. arrived for duty. Sm In92 In V.S. Shepher arrd. In V.07 Struck gone.	752

NO. 1 COMPANY. 41ST DIVISIONAL TRAIN.

WAR DIARY
or
INTELLIGENCE SUMMARY.
(Erase heading not required.)

Army Form C. 2118.

Place	Date	Hour	Summary of Events and Information	Remarks and references to Appendices
COURTRAL	29/10/18		Refd 07.30.	
			Emb: arrived K COURTRAI Stables known by Lieut Trentford	
			Lieut BOSSEGHEM Sick about 10.45.	
			Cpl. T/259640 Dr. MACKERETH A attd to ASC Tank S/cpl.	
			No. T/239902 " NEVILLE J "	
			No. 18117 Cpl. KEYTE B " Isolay Sub 228 Employment Cos	
			No. 257306 Dr. DEAN B " "	
			No. 202201 Dr. WILSON J " (Disagreement) United 105 Field Cos 18th Div Fce 13A	
Do.	30/10/18		Refd O.R.D. No. T3 Sgt. HARWOOD D.W. Stranded G E.C.S a 27E	13B
			Cpl. struck M/Cycle M/O24.242 Expected 1st Line transport of 105 Middlesex	
			Regt (Survey) Isolar fire. Railhead 14.30.	
Do.	31/10/18		Refd 08.00. Railhead 15.15. Isolar fire.	14A

Alexander Trager
O.C. 1 Cmp ANS 41st Divsnl Train.

WAR DIARY
or
INTELLIGENCE SUMMARY.
(Erase heading not required.)

Army Form C. 2118.

NO. 1 COMPANY,
41ST
DIVISIONAL TRAIN.

Instructions regarding War Diaries and Intelligence Summaries are contained in F. S. Regs., Part II. and the Staff Manual respectively. Title pages will be prepared in manuscript.

Place	Date	Hour	Summary of Events and Information	Remarks and references to Appendices
COURTRAI	1/11/18		Refuel 08:00. Supplies drawn by Coys Kanghoh BISSEGHEM railhead 15.15. No: TASK a/Bd. POSKITT, W. Koestend to 4th Army Auxiliary Horse Coys Coy p. & Struck. No: 7418HS Dr: BUTLER, G. H. Corm and ly attached to Wo. 2 Coys. Train Evacuated to C.C.S. Struck W (29/10/18). No. 2 Slememunt (Rec: h 29/10/18) Evacuated to Struck W (debib) Weather fine.	TSS
Do	2/11/18		No refill. Coys arm drawn to Camp a COURTRAI – SNEVEGHEM Road 11:00. 1st Line standing full-up. Weather fine.	TSS
COURTRAI – SNEVEGHEM Road	3/11/18		Supplies drawn from railhead by M.T. Refilled over Camp at 08:30. Weather fine.	TSS
Do	4/11/18		Refill of No. 2 Infy: Coys arm drawn at 10:30 to STEENBRUGGE area. No: S/4253. Pte: GRIFFITHS, R. Evacuated to 2nd Canadian C.C.S. Dr. 17/10/18. & Struck off. Weather fine.	TSS

WAR DIARY
or
INTELLIGENCE SUMMARY.
(Erase heading not required.)

Army Form C. 2118.

NO. 1 COMPANY.
41ST
DIVISIONAL TRAIN.

Place	Date	Hour	Summary of Events and Information	Remarks and references to Appendices
STEENBRUGGE AREA.	5/11/18		Supplies delivered by M.T. Refilled over dump 08.45. Stables 13.30.	108/
Do.	6/11/18		Refill from M.T. 09.00. Stables fine.	108/
DEERLYK AREA.	7/11/18		Refill at B.W.P. Company moved to DEERLYK area at about 10.45. On GRAY H. AMMOCOL to 140 F.A. Bde. Stables fine.	108/
Do.	8/11/18		Refill from M.T. 06.00 at 16.30. No. 73 Wagons on M.T. Convoy from Aec Near Dijt & Taken 8 Length. Mules Shoving. E.Q.M.S. MILLS W. 08299 to 1st Line Shoving.	108/
Do.	9/11/18		Supplies drawn by M.T. from Outland at VICHTE 16.30. Refill in Battn 18.00. 904TH/ 8498695 S/C GRAY H. Evacuated to 64th C.C.S. Sick. Stables fine.	108/
INGOYGHEM AREA.	10/11/18		Company moved to INGOYGHEM area. Refill from M.T. at 20.00. Stables fine.	108/

T2134. Wt. W708—776. 500000. 4/15. Str J. C. & S.

WAR DIARY or INTELLIGENCE SUMMARY

Army Form C. 2118.

No. 1 COMPANY.
41st DIVISIONAL TRAIN.

Place	Date	Hour	Summary of Events and Information	Remarks and references to Appendices
SCHOORISSE AREA	13/11/18		Company ordered to SCHOORISSE area. Supplies delivered to camp by S.A.C. Wgn. at 02:00. Night 11-12. Rations. Very Wet.	
Do.	14/11/18		Rained all day. O.O. No. 7/01 A/S.M. BEACH. J. Rayford to 140 B.C. + Block off (Int. Remained with Coy) No:- 1/S.S.M. HERRY A.R. Ranford Coy to No. 9 Coy. Weather fine.	
Do.	15/11/18		Left 06:00 hrs to No. 116 Division Suie	
NEDERBRAKEL	14/11/18		Left at a 13th Inst. Company arrived at NEDERBRAKEL. Supplies for M.T. + Our Corps + Infantry Issued NR:- 1/SSM BEACH. J. good Weather fine. a/S.S.M. BEACH J. good 140E	
Do.	15/11		Refilled at 11:30 from M.T. Weather fine	

WAR DIARY
or
INTELLIGENCE SUMMARY.

(Erase heading not required.)

Army Form C. 2118.

No. 1 COMPANY.
41ST DIVISIONAL TRAIN.

Place	Date	Hour	Summary of Events and Information	Remarks and references to Appendices
NEDERBRAKEL	16/1/18		Refilled as on 15th instant. Weather fine.	
do	17/1/18		Refilled as on 15th. 1 N.O. Horse (No.32) deducted to 52nd M.V.S. No.106500 Pte VAUGHAN E. and No.632178 Pte JONES H. attached from .238 Employment Coy. Weather fine.	
LUST	18/1/18		Company moved to LUST. 1 N.O. (Motor) deducted to 52nd M.V.S. 2 N.O. Horses received from remount and taken on strength. Weather wet.	
do	19/1/18		Refilled from M.T. at 09.00 hours. 3 N.O. Horses (No.40,No.42,52) where ted as on 18th 1st Struck off the Strength. Weather fine.	
do	20/1/18		Refilled as on 19th instant. Weather fine. TW200203 Q.CULPIN R. attached to 138 Field Ambulance.	
do	21/1/18		Refilled as on 19th instant. Weather fine.	

Army Form C. 2118.

NO. 1 COMPANY.
41ST DIVISIONAL TRAIN.

WAR DIARY
or
INTELLIGENCE SUMMARY.
(Erase heading not required.)

* Instructions regarding War Diaries and Intelligence Summaries are contained in F. S. Regs., Part II. and the Staff Manual respectively. Title pages will be prepared in manuscript.

Place	Date	Hour	Summary of Events and Information	Remarks and references to Appendices
LUS.T	22/1/18		Refilled as on 19th instant. Weather fine	
do	23/1/18		Refilled as on 19th instant. Weather fine	
do	24/1/18		Refilled as on 19th instant. 2 N.O. Horses received from return to unit. Taken on Strength. Weather fine	
do	25/1/18		Refilled as on 19th instant. 1 N.O. Horse (No 32) returned from 53rd M.V.S. taken on Strength. Weather fine	
do	26/1/18		Refilled at 11 am. 10/6626263 Pte CULPIN R evacuated to 606.S on 25/1/18. Struck off Strength. Weather fine	
do	27/1/18		Refilled at 0800 hours. Weather fine	
do	28/1/18		Refilled as on 27th. Weather fine	

Army Form C. 2118.

WAR DIARY
or
INTELLIGENCE SUMMARY.

(Erase heading not required.)

NO. 1 COMPANY,
41ST
DIVISIONAL TRAIN.
No................
Date..............

Instructions regarding War Diaries and Intelligence Summaries are contained in F. S. Regs., Part II. and the Staff Manual respectively. Title pages will be prepared in manuscript.

Place	Date	Hour	Summary of Events and Information	Remarks and references to Appendices
LUST.	29/11		Refilled, as on 24th. Weather fine	
do	30/11		Refilled, as on 24th. Weather fine	

a.a. 1/12/15 No. 1 Coy. 41st Divl Train

WAR DIARY
or
INTELLIGENCE SUMMARY.
(Erase heading not required.)

Army Form C. 2118.

No. 1 COMPANY,
41st
DIVISIONAL TRAIN.

Place	Date	Hour	Summary of Events and Information	Remarks and references to Appendices
LUST	1/1/18		Refll. at 0900 hours from M.T. Weather fine	
do	2/1/18		Refll. as on 1st. Weather fine	
do	3/1/18		Refll. as on 1st. 10946L95 Pte Jones W (Atd from 23rd Empl Coy) Evacuated to CCS on 25/1/18 Sick of Weather fine	
do	4/1/18		Refll. as on 1st. Weather fine	
do	5/1/18		Refll. as on 1st. Weather fine	
do	6/1/18		Refll. as on 1st. Weather fine	
do	7/1/18		Refll. as on 1st. Weather fine	
do	8/1/18		Refll. as on 1st. Weather fine	

Army Form C. 2118.

No. 1 COMPANY,
41st
DIVISIONAL TRAIN.

WAR DIARY
or
INTELLIGENCE SUMMARY.
(Erase heading not required.)

Instructions regarding War Diaries and Intelligence Summaries are contained in F. S. Regs., Part II. and the Staff Manual respectively. Title pages will be prepared in manuscript.

Place	Date	Hour	Summary of Events and Information	Remarks and references to Appendices
LUST	9/10/18		Refilled at 1000hrs No 14/322204 Cpl KENDALL. S. H. transferred from 103 Coy to Fld Amb. No T4/182 L/Cpl KIRK. J transferred to 103 Company. Weather fine	
do	10/10/18		Refilled at 0900 hours. Weather fine	
do	11/10/18		Refilled at 0900 hours. No T4/322219 Pte LYONS. M. No T4/315700 Pte NICHOLSON E. J. No T4/262861 Pte HAMPSHIRE C. and No T4/436601 Pte THORPE J. Joined from 46th Base Depot. taking our strength to T4/190495. Pte GRAY H. H. Invalided from Hospital on S/O list. No 236014 Pte BELL W. attached Nov 235 employment Coy. Weather wet	
VIANE	B/18		Company moved to VIANE. Refilled at 1030 hours. Weather Wet.	

Army Form C. 2118.

NO. 1 COMPANY.
41ST DIVISIONAL TRAIN.
To ....
Date ....

WAR DIARY
or
INTELLIGENCE SUMMARY.
(Erase heading not required.)

Instructions regarding War Diaries and Intelligence Summaries are contained in F. S. Regs., Part II. and the Staff Manual respectively. Title pages will be prepared in manuscript.

Place	Date	Hour	Summary of Events and Information	Remarks and references to Appendices
TUBIZE	13th		Company moved to TUBIZE to refit. Weather showery	
BRAINE-LE-CHATEAU	14th		Refitted at 0830. Company moved to BRAINE-LE-CHATEAU. Weather fine	
do	15th		Refitted at 0830 hours. Weather fine	
BRAINE-LE-HALLEAU	16th		Refitted at 0830 hours. Company moved to BRAINE-LE-HALLEAU. Weather fine	
QUATRE BRAS	17th		Refitted at 0830 hours. Company moved to QUATRE BRAS. Weather fine.	
BOIGNEE	18th		Company moved to BOIGNEE. Refugees at Hootumps. Wet	
EGHEZEE	19th		Refitted at 0830 hours. Company moved to EGHEZEE. Fine	

WAR DIARY
or
INTELLIGENCE SUMMARY

Army Form C. 2118.

No. 1 COMPANY,
41st DIVISIONAL TRAIN.

Place	Date	Hour	Summary of Events and Information	Remarks and references to Appendices
FUNAL	20/1/19		Refilled at 0830 hours. Company moved to FUNAL. Weather Wet	
do	21/1/19		Refilled at 1000 hours. Forage 1/S.S.M Hutt. S.D. Attached from H.Q. 41st Div. Train, on Return't	
HUY	22/1/19		Subfees arrive from Railhead HUY at 800 hrs have transport. Weather fine. Coy moved to HUY	
do	23/1/19		Railhead at 800 hours. 10783 Mayre Dr GETJENS T. and 81/30398 Dr WHITE F.H. (on leave) proceeded to England. Weather Showery	
do	24/1/19		Railhead at 800 hours. Weather Wet. Snow.	
do	25/1/19		Railhead no one 24th.	

WAR DIARY or INTELLIGENCE SUMMARY

Army Form C. 2118.

No. 1 COMPANY.
41ST DIVISIONAL TRAIN.

Place	Date	Hour	Summary of Events and Information	Remarks and references to Appendices
HUY	July 26/15		Rail head as on 24th. 2 W.O.'s joined for duty. Horses & personnel — Strength of Strength. Weather fine.	
do	27/7/15		Rail head as on 24th. Weather fine.	
do	28/7/15		Rail head as on 24th. Weather wet.	
do	29/7/15		Rail head at 1500 yards. 10/1235/15 Dr. BOWES, T. admitted to 110 Field Ambulance.	
do	30/7/15		Rail head at 0900 yards. 1140 Horse (10/12) Sergeant A attached to No 2 Coy. Wm. returned on termination of attachment. Casualty 6SM RILEY. P.S. admitted to 110 Field Ambulance. No 75615? Dr. MAIR, R. admitted to Military Hospital PR whilst on leave. L/Sergt A/Sergt from 2H.S. Cavalry Reserve L. 17/11/36/7. dt. 26/7/1915. Weather showery.	

Army Form C. 2118.

NO. 1 COMPANY,
41ST
DIVISIONAL TRAIN.

WAR DIARY
or
INTELLIGENCE SUMMARY.
(Erase heading not required.)

Instructions regarding War Diaries and Intelligence Summaries are contained in F. S. Regs., Part II. and the Staff Manual respectively. Title pages will be prepared in manuscript.

Place	Date	Hour	Summary of Events and Information	Remarks and references to Appendices
HUY	3/1/19		Railhead at 800 yards. The following Coal Miners proceeded to U.K. for demobilization this day:- 14/25100 Pte Nicholson E. 145/03857 Pte Thomas T. 173/43 Sigr Pte Marsden T. 13/31319 Pte Wilson PR. Weather fine.	

A.C. Hd. Qrs. SOY. 41st DIVL TRAIN.

WAR DIARY or **INTELLIGENCE SUMMARY.**

Army Form C. 2118.

No 1603

Place	Date	Hour	Summary of Events and Information	Remarks and references to Appendices
HUY	1/1/19		Railhead at 0900 hours. No TW/123145 Pte BOWES L. evacuated to 50 CCS on 31/12/18 - Sick at Strength. No P. NOBLE (10 HM) died on 29.30 Dec. (see died at other.) Sick 10 ARMY Weather fine.	A.M.
do	2/1/19		Railhead as on 1st. No 20 1523 Pte LOVELL T. (of 23S team p (Loyt)) rejoined from detention camp(s) taken on Strength. Weather fine.	A.M.
do	3/1/19		Railhead as on 1st. No T/336614 Pte HIGHLEY A.G. joined from R.A.S.C. (now Corps Rebel Value) taken on Strength. Weather Snowy.	A.M.
do	4/1/19		Railhead at 0830 am. No TW5 Mears. 10/17604 Pte DANIEL E.G; 10/18505 Pte DAWSON H.A.; T/491817 Pte EVANS G.; T/04001 Pte GEOR J James. T/08103 Pte WATSON Pte rejoined from 24 1/2 rein camp on 21/3 taken on Strength. No T/259416 Pte RILEY P.S dislocated knee. W.O 24/12 Old Ambulance. Weather fine.	A.M.

Army Form C. 2118.

No. 1 COMPANY.
41st
SURGICAL TRAIN.

WAR DIARY
or
INTELLIGENCE SUMMARY.

(Erase heading not required.)

Instructions regarding War Diaries and Intelligence Summaries are contained in F. S. Regs., Part II. and the Staff Manual respectively. Title pages will be prepared in manuscript.

Place	Date	Hour	Summary of Events and Information	Remarks and references to Appendices
10Y	5/19		Railroad at 0800 hours. Rolles' Pte JONES W. (635 Emp Coy) relieved from Labour Coy to Base Depot Calais sick. Pte P/3335 Pte CARTER W. evac. to hospital at 2815 hrs sick at spit (No 2363) Pte CULPIN R. G/9-111334 Pte CROOME J (635 emp coy) to Muck from Steenbroke dug 3/19 severe cough. Weather fine	AM
do	6/19		Pulling at R. road. 1 O.R. evac (No 5) evacuated Strach No 0 H Brught Weather fine	AM
do	7/19		Supplies drawn from Railhead AMBIN at 0830 hours.	AM
do	8/19		Railhead as on 7th. Weather fine.	AM
do	9/19		Railhead as on 7th. Weather fine	AM

WAR DIARY
or
INTELLIGENCE SUMMARY.

Army Form C. 2118.

Place	Date	Hour	Summary of Events and Information	Remarks and references to Appendices
HUY	10/19		Railhead open. Visit T/Captain E.M. WOOD demobilised, whilst on leave up. A/Capt of the Staff from 20.12.18. 1st & 2nd Nov (10.10) died on 28th December 18. Struck off Strength. Weather fine.	A.M.
	16/11/19		Railroad working. Weather fine.	A.M.
	17/11/19		Ry head at 0800 hours. Weather fine.	A.M.
	13/10		Railhead as on 12th, not admitted to Canadian Field Ambulance. 2nd Lt R RUSSELL attached. Weather fine.	A.M.
	20/10/19		Railhead as on 12th, not W/556 Dr GODWIN D joined from 102 Group 102. 2nd Lt O area Reception Camp. Weather fine.	A.M.

WAR DIARY
or
INTELLIGENCE SUMMARY.
(Erase heading not required.)

Army Form C. 2118.

No. 1 COMPANY,
4 T gr
DIVISION_TRAIN.

Place	Date	Hour	Summary of Events and Information	Remarks and references to Appendices
HUY	5/9		Company detrained at HUY Station. Weather fine	A/M
GERMANY KALK	16/9		Company detrained WITH N marched to Billets at KALK. 1st Lieut G.W. GREY was demobilised. W.R. Strength on 23/9/15. Whilst on Route. Weather fine	A/M
do	1/10		Refilled from M.T. at KALK at 0800 hours. Weather fine	A/M
do	5/10		Refill as on 1st. Weather fine	A/M
do	10/10		Refilled at 0900 hours. Weather fine	A/M
do	20/10		Refill as on 10th. Weather fine	A/M

WAR DIARY
or
INTELLIGENCE SUMMARY.
(Erase heading not required.)

Army Form C. 2118.

No. 1 COMPANY,
41st
DIVISIONAL TRAIN.

Place	Date	Hour	Summary of Events and Information	Remarks and references to Appendices
KOLK	21/6	0800	Refilled at 0800 hours T/4/88266 Dr Russell T. Durcharged from 50th CCS	Weather fine AM
do	22/6		Refill as on 21st 1/32010 N/SSM HULL J.M. (Katchd) transferred to 1st Cavalry Division HT Sect	Weather fine AM
do	23/6		Refill as on 21st 10/28547 Pte FRY E (Katchd) from 238 Company) admitted 146 field amb.	Weather fine
do	24/6		Refill as on 21st T/3/6162 Dr WALKER J. admitted to 146 fd amb. T/4/84465 Dr GREEN S. proceeded to UK on demobilisation. Struck off strength 2nd Horses (1183+152) admitted to 52 DVS	Weather fine AM
do	25/6		Refill as on 21st T/ Musgrave Dr PARKES SE admitted 146 fd Ambulance	Weather fine AM

WAR DIARY
or
INTELLIGENCE SUMMARY.

Army Form C. 2118.

Place	Date	Hour	Summary of Events and Information	Remarks and references to Appendices
KoLK	26/10		Roll Call on 21st. Weather fine	AM
do	27/10		Refill Coy on 21st. No report for Coy. Strength of Coy. No. 606 1. Strength of Coy. 1.W. No. 1039 56 Pte BRADLEY F.C. No. 1120263 Pte HUNT W. were admitted to W. field Ambulance. (No. 1113153) were evacuated. Strength of Coy that instant	Sailes J.E. evacuated to W. field Ambulance Pte CROCKFORD 2/1.O. HOPPER AM
do	28/10		Supplies drawn from Railhead. Pte L.T. at 09hrs hours. No. 191516 Pte SEED J. + No. 201523 Pte GREGORY W.1333(arty coy) were admitted to W. field Ambulance. No. 155782 Pte WALKER T. was evacuated to 666 on 35 K. Strength of Strength oc that date	AM
do	29/10		Railhead GR on 28th. No. 125643 Sgt SMITH G. No. 63575 Pte JONES H. + No. 100063 Pte LAIRD D. admitted to W. field Amb. Weather fine.	AM

WAR DIARY or INTELLIGENCE SUMMARY

Army Form C. 2118.

No. 1 COMPANY, 41ST DIVISIONAL TRAIN.

Place	Date	Hour	Summary of Events and Information	Remarks and references to Appendices
KALK	30/6		Supplies drawn from Railhead. HEUMOR at arr. hours & 1500 hours. T/3/4031 Pte RENALDSON M, 5/055123 Pte McKAY W, 20151 Pte COLLIER C.L. admitted to No. 2 field Ambulance. T/0166/15 Pte COPPING R (Att) No. 235 (part pay) Detached to LR. On 28/10. Strength this WR kept. T/03/890 Pte BAKER W was evacuated to No. 163 two days. Weather fine.	MM
	31/6		Supplies drawn from Railhead at arr. hours & 1500 hours. W/18186 L/Cpl OSBORNE T.S., T/5/9250 Dvr CHRISTIAN W and W/9315 Pte SCARLETT W were admitted to No. 2 field Ambulance. T/4/03438 Dvr BRADLEY E.C. & No. 2235M Pte FRY E. 49 N.C. discharged from No. 2 field. Weather fine.	MM

Mitchley B Major
For O.C. No. 1 Coy 41st Divl. Train.

Army Form C. 2118.

NO. 1 COMPANY,
41ST
DIVISIONAL TRAIN.

WAR DIARY
or
INTELLIGENCE SUMMARY.
(Erase heading not required.)

Instructions regarding War Diaries and Intelligence Summaries are contained in F. S. Regs., Part II. and the Staff Manual respectively. Title pages will be prepared in manuscript.

Place	Date	Hour	Summary of Events and Information	Remarks and references to Appendices
KOLK	2/1/19		Supplies drawn from Railhead HEUMAR at 10.15 hours 10/WS600 lbs. Section 1. Proceeded to lok. for Denue Pilgatory. At © Norge 10128 evacuated from Nr 18 Stuck of Studhy town 30/1A 19/0453. L/Cpl. OSBORNE T.S. discharged from No 18 and No. No. 085835 Pt. MERRYWEATHER W.G. W.S. admitted to No 16 F.A.	Weather fine
do	2/1/19		Supplies as on 1st.	Snow
do	3/1/19		Supplies as on 1st. 21 O'Heres Mod. (ored) were evacuated en 3/1/19 Stuck of Stong. Ho from that date 10/00/12 Pr. YOUNG 1. (Organizing Dr. McCann) Wr.3 N306641 Dr. WALKER J. 10.20/141 the THORNTON H (253 Emp.Coy) were admitted to No 16 Field Amb. 10/0.32/158 Pr. JONES H. also from dept.	Snow

WAR DIARY
or
INTELLIGENCE SUMMARY.

(Erase heading not required.)

Army Form C. 2118.

No. 1 COMPANY,
41st
DIVISIONAL TRAIN.

Place	Date	Hour	Summary of Events and Information	Remarks and references to Appendices
KALK	1/6/19		Supplies as on 1st. Cpl W/283685 Coll WHITE D; T/424383 Dr Gilbert J; T/415501 Dr GOODINGS L; 9 Jt/22632 Dr PURCHASE D.E. were admitted to 116 Field Amb. Weather fine	Alt
do	5/6/19		Supplies as on 1st. 10/15266 Lcpl to Cpl Rankins F.W deceased. 10/11635 Dr McLOUGHLIN M admitted to 116 Field Amb (mumps). T/30747 Pte THORNTON H (21st Inf. Coy) (returned to 66852 Pte St Skeugh. Weather fine	Alt
do	18/6/19		Supplies as on 1st. Weather fine	Alt

WAR DIARY
or
INTELLIGENCE SUMMARY

(Erase heading not required.)

Army Form C. 2118.

NO. 1 COMPANY.
41ST DIVISIONAL TRAIN.

Place	Date	Hour	Summary of Events and Information	Remarks and references to Appendices
KALK	1/1/19		Supplies as on 1st.	
			07/3169135 Sgt Smith G died on 1st squadron to GS on 5 inst.	
			011172316 Pte Andrews C admitted to field ambulance	
			014212 Dr Seep J (came to GS 3/14) to 13603 Dr Ronaldson M)	
			010028/63 Pte Hunt W { to GS 6/3/19 (came to GS 6/19)	
			0152256 Pte Christian W { to GS 6/3/19 Pte McKay W (came to GS 6/19)	
			0702236 Pte Merryweather W { came to GS 1/19 0766/83 Pte Laird R (came to GS)	
			023816 Dr Walker J { 0201583 " Gregory W (on 5th)	
			0201511 " Collier C.	
			0236107 Bell W.) on 21/19	
			All the above have been struck off strength from date shown.	
			Weather fine	
3	2/1/19		Supplies as on 1st. 1st to Depot Pk Kidney Ct (GS Employ)	
			discharged from UK	
			1/NZ/100 Sent to 32nd MTS	
			Weather fine	

WAR DIARY
or
INTELLIGENCE SUMMARY.
(Erase heading not required.)

Army Form C. 2118.

NO. 1 COMPANY,
41ST
DIVISIONAL TRAIN.

Place	Date	Hour	Summary of Events and Information	Remarks and references to Appendices
Kalk	9/1/19		Supplies as per 1st No T/O97/12 Pte Young T. discharged from H.R. and No 14315 Pte Scarlett W. (339 Comp Coy) discharged from H.B.	MK
do	10/1/19		Supplies as per 1st M Intake. Pte Andrews C. discharged from Hospital. T/2/101 Pte Newey H. evacuated to 163°v's th & R.O. Horses received from 139 Field Amb. Taken on Strength.	Weather fine. MK
do	11/1/19		Supplies as per 1st No T/W/33685 Cpl White D., T/2586 Pte Godwin A, No T/3/2199 Pte McCann N Jy T/11501 Pte Goddings L. were discharged from Hospital	Weather fine. MK

WAR DIARY
or
INTELLIGENCE SUMMARY.

(Erase heading not required.)

Army Form C. 2118.

NO. 1 COMPANY.
41ST
DIVISIONAL TRAIN.

Place	Date	Hour	Summary of Events and Information	Remarks and references to Appendices
KALK	12/2/19		Supplies as usual. No/32323R Dr. PURCHASE. A.E. discharged from Hospital. The undermentioned were transferred from unit as stated. T4/ taken on Strength. T4/045364 Sgt Davis E.H.) T4/ 1ms to Pr. DAWES B.W. T4/-245127 Dr. BUCKMASTER S.J.) from 110 + B. T4/ 103326 Dr Flight W.H. T4/ 051416 Dr Jefferson C.H. from 1Sq T.M. T4/ Sieg Dr Palmer J. Weather fine	Nil
do	13/19		Supplies as on 1st. No/41569 Dr POMER J admitted to No 1 B. To/ 102828 Dr GILBERT J. evacuated to 6 6 8 11Sg & Struck off Streng R. To/ 13/02/051 Dr RONOLDON M. rejoined from 6 6 8 12 7/9 taken own Strength R. Weather fine	Nil

Army Form C. 2118.

No. 1 COMPANY,
41st
DIVISIONAL TRAIN.

WAR DIARY
or
INTELLIGENCE SUMMARY.
(Erase heading not required.)

Instructions regarding War Diaries and Intelligence Summaries are contained in F. S. Regs., Part II. and the Staff Manual respectively. Title pages will be prepared in manuscript.

Place	Date	Hour	Summary of Events and Information	Remarks and references to Appendices
KALK	14/9/19		Supplies as on 1st. No. 16616 Pte McLoughlin M evacuated to 66s 137/g sick of Sick. K. cigarest Pte Ronaldson M was admitted to No 17 F.D. Pte P Yore (No 100) was destroyed as 35 M.I.S on 10/9/19 x Struck off Strength (Weather fine.)	M
	15/9/19		Supplies as on 1st. (Weather wet)	M
	16/9/19		Supplies as on 1st. No 172600 Pte Shorter F. K. to G. W.H.Q.W. train. No 130654 Pte Walker J. to 111 F. K. S. at Newey H. returned from 36 C.C.S on 15/9 x taken on Strength (Weather fine)	M

WAR DIARY
or
INTELLIGENCE SUMMARY.
(Erase heading not required.)

Army Form C. 2118.

No. 1 COMPANY,
41st
DIVISIONAL TRAIN.

Place	Date	Hour	Summary of Events and Information	Remarks and references to Appendices
KOLK	17/9		Supplies to Div. 1st. No. 065330 Dr SORE J.W. transferred from Div. Field Ambulance on 15/9 is taken on strength. No 391894 Pte SWEENEY J.P. (235 Inf Bde) proceded to LR for demobilisation on 16/9 to Sheffield Strength. Weather fine	M
do	18/9		Supplies as on 1st. No M/5160 Dr NAPIER J and No 202069 Pte JONES J (239 Inf Bde) were discharged from hospital. Weather fine	M
do	19/9		Supplies to Div. 1st. No M/316213 A/S/Sgt Jones B.W. transferred from MAS Sheffield Strength. The following were taken on strength from Div. Field Ambulance. No T5/4605 S/Sgt Powell J. No T/315501 W.O. DIPRIOR D. T5/6479 W.O. AT JA KLUGTON W.C. Weather fine	M

WAR DIARY
or
INTELLIGENCE SUMMARY.
(Erase heading not required.)

Army Form C. 2118.

No. 1 COMPANY,
41st
DIVISIONAL TRAIN.

Place	Date	Hour	Summary of Events and Information	Remarks and references to Appendices
KALK	20/1/19		Supplies as on 1st. 1/S Lieut C.J. Bloodworth Mott & Lieut Shepherd A were transferred from 2nd Cavalry Divisional Base, taken on strength. The following proceeded to UK for demobilization & are struck off strength. T/30208 S/Sjt. Gibb WH, T/316 Cpl. Brown WH, T/324449 Pte McCann WJ, T/4752629 Dr. Duckmanton SJ, T/4172316 Dr. Manners WR. Weather fine	AF
do	21/1/19		Supplies as on 1st. Weather fine	AF
do	22/1/19		Supplies as on 1st. Weather fine	AF
do	23/1/19		Supplies as on 1st. Weather fine	AF
do	24/1/19		Supplies as on 1st. Lt. 13/0231 Dr Rennyson M. were discharged from 1/5 Field Ambulance. Weather wet	AF

WAR DIARY
INTELLIGENCE SUMMARY
(Erase heading not required.)

Army Form C. 2118.

NO. 1 COMPANY,
41st
DIVISIONAL TRAIN.

Place	Date	Hour	Summary of Events and Information	Remarks and references to Appendices
KALK	9/6/19		Supplies as on 1st. 10/05/2118 Pr Bowden R. was admitted to 110 field Ambulance. No 53144 Private FITZSIMONS P. of 355/11 A.E. HORDY H.N. attacked 238 Employment Coy. 2 N.R. Stores (Nos MT 58) were admitted to 53rd M.L.S. Weather showery	A/f
do	20/6/19		Supplies as on 1st. 2/Captain C.C. BELL M.C.R.A.S.C. (F.A.D.) joined on 25th from 110th Divisional Train. is taking on Strength. Weather fine	A/f
do	21/6/19		Supplies as on 1st. No 15 L/Cpl Mees W.A. L/Cpl POWELL J. was evacuated to 110 Sty 23/11 Y No 146 5218 Pr Bowman R. was evacuated on 26/19 and Church of England Strength. No 2586 Pr CROPPIN A. was admitted to 110 field ambulance. Weather fine	A/f

Army Form C. 2118.

NO. 1 COMPANY.
41ST
DIVISIONAL TRAIN.

WAR DIARY
or
INTELLIGENCE SUMMARY.
(Erase heading not required.)

Place	Date	Hour	Summary of Events and Information	Remarks and references to Appendices
KOLK	25/2/16		Supplies as for 1st (or 75) /1605 Shalby Powell 1st (Dec the same	1/1
			Drawn in 21st Coy S	
			Memorizp L	
			1. Ob /o/ Coy 41st Divl train	

WAR DIARY
or
INTELLIGENCE SUMMARY.
(Erase heading not required.)

Army Form C. 2118.

Place	Date	Hour	Summary of Events and Information	Remarks and references to Appendices
KOLK	1/3/19		Supplies drawn from Railhead. No 2208 Pt GREEN A.E admitted to 1st Western General Troops Hosp. whilst on leave via Stuch & Shingly from 13/1/19. The following joined as leaders from 235 Employment Coy 12118 L/Cpl HEDGES E; 51045 Pte BOOTH H; 68521 Pte FENTON S.H; 64419 Pte SMART C.R.	Weather fine. 00°F
do	2/3/19		Supplies as on 1st. No 17356 Pt GODWIN D declared from H.to held Ambylance. No 11334 Prite GREEN J (238 Emp. Coy) demobilized whilst on leave. Stuck of Ham from 26/1/19. 2 NO Herses (MR-58) evacuated & Stuck of Ham 20/3/19.	Weather fine. 00°F
do	3/3/19		Supplies as on 1st. 1 NO Horse (MKSO) evacuated & Stuck of Ham 30/49	Wea fr Showery 00°F

WAR DIARY
or
INTELLIGENCE SUMMARY.
(Erase heading not required.)

Army Form C. 2118.

Place	Date	Hour	Summary of Events and Information	Remarks and references to Appendices
KALK	3/7/19		Supplies as on 1st.	Weather fine. GGR
do	4/7/19		Supplies as on 1st.	Weather fine. GGR
do	5/7/19		Supplies drawn from Railhead HEUDER at 0900 hours. No 438101 Pte THORPE J. Tw. & 6530 Dr SPRULE T.N proceeded to U.K. for demobilization. Struck off Strength. No 204618 Pte BLUNDELL F. & T/433963 Pte JONES D.H transferred from Spare No Quarters.	Weather fine. GGR
do	6/7/19		Supplies as on 1st. No 15/861 Sjt Dr PRIOR D. was discharged from No 2 Field Ambulance.	Weather fine. GGR

WAR DIARY
or
INTELLIGENCE SUMMARY.
(Erase heading not required.)

Army Form C. 2118.

Place	Date	Hour	Summary of Events and Information	Remarks and references to Appendices
KOLK	8/9		Supplies as on 6th. 2 N.C.O.'s (Sergts) and 1 Pte (No.12) were attached to 62nd M.V.S. Weather Showery	COE
do	9/9		Supplies as on 6th. 10 O.R.'s W.O.A. Pocklington M.C. discharged from 1/1 Fd Ambulance. Weather fine.	COE
do	10/9		Supplies as on 6th. Weather fine.	COE
do	11/9		Supplies as per 6th. 1 Rider (No.12) & 2 H.D. Horses (Nos 49 & 118) evacuated & struck off the strength. Weather fine.	COE

Army Form C. 2118.

WAR DIARY
or
INTELLIGENCE SUMMARY.
(Erase heading not required.)

Instructions regarding War Diaries and Intelligence Summaries are contained in F. S. Regs., Part II. and the Staff Manual respectively. Title pages will be prepared in manuscript.

Place	Date	Hour	Summary of Events and Information	Remarks and references to Appendices
KALK	12/3/19		Supplies as on 6" inst	Weather fine	CoR
do	13/3/19		Supplies as on 6" inst	Weather fine	CoR
do	14/3/19		Supplies as on 6" inst	Weather fine	CoR
do	15/3/19		Supplies as on 6" inst	Weather fine	CoR
do	16/3/19		Supplies as on 6" inst. 2 Riders (Nos. 9 & 14) & 1 H.P. horse (No. 51) evacuated & struck off the strength. Sig. Halliday, N.Z. proceeded to N.Z. for demobilization & struck off the strength. Weather fine	CoR

WAR DIARY
~~INTELLIGENCE SUMMARY~~
(Erase heading not required.)

Army Form C. 2118.

Place	Date	Hour	Summary of Events and Information	Remarks and references to Appendices
Kirk	17/9		Supplies as on the 6 inst. During temporary absence of Major Cosgray at Basrah Lt. Tukorees officer of S. & T. Elicit Supplies from 18 inst. Weather fine	OOK
do	18/9		Supplies as on 6 inst. Our Remounts & Animals supplied with supplies from 18/9/19 & 19/9/19 from 10/9/19 to 15/9/19. Our /Mr.Hydromette 140 & 7R & Weather fine	OOK
do	19/9		Supplies as on 6 inst. A. T.& G.M. Lele of Cheshires to our 2nd Div. 2nd FM Mortydell for the purpose of buying ?. Weather fine.	OOK
do	20/9		Supplies as on 6 inst. 1 I.O.(M.F.O) evacuated. Struck off the strength. Weather fine	OOK

WAR DIARY
or
INTELLIGENCE SUMMARY.

Army Form C. 2118.

(Erase heading not required.)

Instructions regarding War Diaries and Intelligence Summaries are contained in F. S. Regs., Part II. and the Staff Manual respectively. Title pages will be prepared in manuscript.

Place	Date	Hour	Summary of Events and Information	Remarks and references to Appendices
Kirkee	21/9		Supplies as on 6' inst. 7357246 Dvr J Whyte discharged from I.F.A. Weather fine	OOR
do.	22/9		Supplies as on 6' inst. Weather fine	OOR
do	23/9		Supplies as on 6' inst. Weather fine	OOR
do	24/9		Supplies as on 6' inst. Weather fine	OOR
do	25/9		Supplies as on the 6 inst. 7356607 Dvr Pike I disc/dis'chd whitewash sent E to H. 1/4/19. 7365-38 Dvr Withers J admitted to No 7 A. Weather fine	OOR

T2134. Wt. W708—776. 500000. 4/15. Sir J. C. & S.

Army Form C. 2118.

WAR DIARY
or
~~INTELLIGENCE SUMMARY~~
(Erase heading not required.)

Instructions regarding War Diaries and Intelligence Summaries are contained in F. S. Regs., Part II. and the Staff Manual respectively. Title pages will be prepared in manuscript.

Place	Date	Hour	Summary of Events and Information	Remarks and references to Appendices
Kalk	26/9		Supplies as on 6th inst. 1/265-3# Pvt. Wilson Erased to CCS struck off the strength. Weather fine	CCR
Do.	27/9		Supplies as on 6th inst. 1 Rider from H. Qrs. 11 East Bgde taken on the strength from 20/9/19. Weather dull (showers)	CCR
Do.	28/9		Supplies as on 6th inst. 3/71342 Dvr Marshall F.W. tried by D.C.M. found guilty & sentenced to 28 days F.P. No 2. Weather dull (showers).	CCR
Do.	29/9		Supplies as on the 6th inst. Weather dull (showers).	CCR

WAR DIARY
or
INTELLIGENCE SUMMARY
(Erase heading not required.)

Army Form C. 2118.

Place	Date	Hour	Summary of Events and Information	Remarks and references to Appendices
Kalk	30/3/19		Supplies as on the 6 inst	cwr
Do	31/3/19	3.00	Supplies as on 6 inst. No 400509 Pte Riley G to Cpl 356145 Pte Thatcher GP having returned to 238 Coy are struck off the strength	wr
			Weather dull (snow)	

Marshall Capt
1/4/19
O.C. No.1 Coy DIVL TRAIN
London

Army Form C. 2118.

WAR DIARY
or
INTELLIGENCE SUMMARY.
(Erase heading not required.)

Instructions regarding War Diaries and Intelligence Summaries are contained in F. S. Regs., Part II. and the Staff Manual respectively. Title pages will be prepared in manuscript.

1 Coy

Place	Date	Hour	Summary of Events and Information	Remarks and references to Appendices
KALK	1/9		Supplies drawn at Deurne at 9 o'clock (Railway) Weather fine	M
do	2/9		Supplies as for 1st. T/40/09/964 Den Hoorn B. admitted to 40 F. Amb. Weather fine	M
do	3/9		Supplies as no 1st Weather fine	M
do	4/9		Supplies as no 1st. T/40/09/230 Pte. Young & T/30/09/982 C.Q.M.S. Millett admitted to 40 F. Amb. 2 Riders from Farm Hdqrs taken in the strength Winter fine	M
			T/4/09/229	
do	5/9		Supplies as no 1:- a/Sgt Cox promoted Sgt. W/165 see T/06/25 Cpl. Sanderson T/6/15/243 a/L/Sgt Knox appointed full see T/9/85 L/Sgt Ryder L.G.M.S. Miller evacuated to the C.C.S. & thence to the Depot. Weather fine	M

T2134. Wt. W708-776. 500000. 4/15. Sir J. C. & S.

Army Form C. 2118.

WAR DIARY
or
INTELLIGENCE SUMMARY.
(Erase heading not required.)

Instructions regarding War Diaries and Intelligence Summaries are contained in F. S. Regs., Part II. and the Staff Manual respectively. Title pages will be prepared in manuscript.

Place	Date	Hour	Summary of Events and Information	Remarks and references to Appendices
KALK	6/9		Supplies as on 1st. Weather fine	M
do	7/9		Supplies as on 2nd. Weather fine	M
do	8/9		Supplies as on 3rd. T/094/23 Dvr Patrick RD evacuated to 31 CCS & struck off the strength. Weather fine	M
do	9/9		Supplies as on 3 inst. T/094/12 Dvr Young discharged from No 2 Ack. Weather fine	M
do	10/9		Supplies as on 3rd inst. Weather fine	M
do	11/9		Supplies as on 3rd inst. The following joined as orders from 238 Coy A Army: 19/16 Pte HANNAH J.S. 239/61 Pte WINGFIELD 635/62 Pte WARD C. 462/32 Pte BUCK M. 266/26 Pte BROWN HA. 282/8 Pte LAVENDER T. 057/618 Pte PALMER E.W. 697/5 Pte RUSSELL G. Weather showery	M

T2134. Wt. W708-776. 500000. 4/15. Sir J. C. & S.

Army Form C. 2118.

WAR DIARY
or
INTELLIGENCE SUMMARY.
(Erase heading not required.)

Instructions regarding War Diaries and Intelligence Summaries are contained in F. S. Regs., Part II. and the Staff Manual respectively. Title pages will be prepared in manuscript.

Place	Date	Hour	Summary of Events and Information	Remarks and references to Appendices
KALK	12/9	17/9	Supplies as on 3rd inst.	Weather Showery
do.	13/9		Supplies as on 3rd inst. The following joined from 5th Divisional Train 1513461 Burbidge J A. T/32596 Fleming W. T/32505 Dyball T/34472 Gray J T/36652 Hancock R.S. T/39192 Kent J.J. T/35466 Lukyn L. 1 C.X. H.D. No 119 destroyed struck off the strength	Weather Showers
do.	14/9		Supplies as on 3rd inst. T/35631 Dar Moles S.O. evacuated to 36 C.C.S.	Weather Showery
do.	15/9		Supplies as on 3rd inst. 363561 Pte Gourlay J. (Driver) joined from 23rd Sympt. Coy.	Weather fair (showery)

WAR DIARY
or
INTELLIGENCE SUMMARY

Army Form C. 2118.

Place	Date	Hour	Summary of Events and Information	Remarks and references to Appendices
KALK	16/7/19		Syphilis cases 3rd inst. The following N.C.O.'s & men joined from Guards Depot Havre - Rowley Cpl A.H.H. W.D. T/8/1/19, Strafford Cpl F.L. T/5/8/19. L/Cpl Y... Perkins Sergt J. T/5/19/83. L/Cpls Ewy Co Evans G/51 T/6/11/19. Dnr Parrish M. 15/06/19. Miller G.H. T/6/11/33. Mason A. T/5/302. Tpr Dr Dale C.J. Weather fine	M
do	17/7/19		Syphilis cases 3rd inst - T/4/19/644 Dnr Evans D. discharged from 100 G. Amb. Weather fine.	M
do	18/7/19		Syphilis cases on 3rd inst - T/6/190,956 Pte Thomas G.R. joined from 23 Empl. Coy. At Kalk on the strength in a troops. Weather fine.	M

WAR DIARY
or
INTELLIGENCE SUMMARY.
(Erase heading not required.)

Army Form C. 2118.

Place	Date	Hour	Summary of Events and Information	Remarks and references to Appendices
KALK	19/9		Supplies as on 3rd inst. Major R.W. Parker sworn in for General Service notation in R. schedule off 5th through twos from 27/3/19	
do	20/9		Supplies as 3rd inst. Mailes from	
do	21/9		Supplies as on 3rd inst. The 91136/46 Dvr Bell H.J. posted from 20 Divisional Train at Cuttoe on Knoll. Whittier Lane	
do	22/9		Supplies as on 3rd inst. The L. Young Driver reposted for Investigation by Struck off str 23519 Pte Brown E.G. 23361 Pte Jay E. 133570 Pte Lamb Joseph G. 102230 Pte Vaughan J. Water Shores	

Army Form C. 2118.

WAR DIARY
or
INTELLIGENCE SUMMARY.
(Erase heading not required.)

Instructions regarding War Diaries and Intelligence Summaries are contained in F. S. Regs., Part II. and the Staff Manual respectively. Title pages will be prepared in manuscript.

Place	Date	Hour	Summary of Events and Information	Remarks and references to Appendices
KALK	23/9		Supplies as on 3rd inst. Weather fine.	M
do	24/9		Supplies as on 3rd inst. Major A. Sadler D.S.O. joined from 4th Division. Train up taken on the strength. Gas from 22/4/9	M
do	25/9		Supplies as on 3rd inst. Weather fine. Weather fine.	M
do	26/9		Supplies as on 3rd inst. The following N.C.O. & men joined proceeded for distribution the strength of the strength. Sergts E.J.M. Luckhurst T.41-735/6, Dr. J. Hughes T.4/075236 On Board M.S. T.3/07706. On enqd. y. Weather fine.	M

Army Form C. 2118.

WAR DIARY
or
INTELLIGENCE SUMMARY.
(Erase heading not required.)

Instructions regarding War Diaries and Intelligence Summaries are contained in F. S. Regs., Part II. and the Staff Manual respectively. Title pages will be prepared in manuscript.

Place	Date	Hour	Summary of Events and Information	Remarks and references to Appendices
KALK	27/9		Supplies as on 3rd inst. 14/28/101 Pr Lewey I./ T/3569. Pr Dighty A.S. admitted to Field Amb. Weather fine.	M
do.	28/9		Supplies as on 3rd inst. Weather dull.	
do.	29/9		Supplies as on 3rd inst. Inter-Di Race Meeting (1st day). Weather dull (showers)	M
do.	30/9		Supplies as on 3rd inst. Inter-Di Race Meeting (2nd day). Weather fine.	M

WAR DIARY
or
INTELLIGENCE SUMMARY.
(Erase heading not required.)

Army Form C. 2118.

Place	Date	Hour	Summary of Events and Information	Remarks and references to Appendices
KALK	1/9		Supplies drawn from Railhead HEUMAR at 09.00 hours. No 201533 Pte Lovell J & No 16bus Pte Kidney G proceeded to 238 "Coy" sent for demob. strength of the strength	Copy
do	2/9		Weather fine. Supplies as on 1st inst. The following ORs proceeded to UK on demob. struck off strength at 7 A.M. Kent L to 1405616 Dr Jerram G M4476 Dr Wynne A T/4/083 Dr West H T/108396 Dr High WJ T/409295 Dr Steel G T/405715 Dr Lyon J T/3/07131 Dr Jenkins AJ T/4/09218 Dr Newton AA T/4/10616 Dr Prior D Weather fine	Copy
do	3/9		Supplies as on 1st inst No 203768 Pte Pope L 238 "Coy Coy taken on the strength Weather fine	Copy
do	4/9		Supplies as on 1st inst Weather fine	Copy

WAR DIARY
or
INTELLIGENCE SUMMARY.

(Erase heading not required.)

Army Form C. 2118.

Place	Date	Hour	Summary of Events and Information	Remarks and references to Appendices
KALK.	3/9		Supplies as on 1st inst. To/046 w/s Dr Alethy O. admitted to 2/Field Amb. Co/.E. T/25536 Pte Wilson G Landry joined from General Base Depot no change in strength.	OOR
do	6/9		Instructions Dr Cooks's link. The following WR's transferred from 29th Grave. One(1) Leut. 8 Other ranks Strength T/06129 A/Cpt Meade S T/2925/6 Pte Bavernost & T/38743 Pte Livery W T/36758 Pte Beaver W T/2oo to Pte Hugh SG. The following WR's having proceeded to 14th Grave One (1) Leut. Strach 8 The Other Ranks T/057661 Dr McCulley S T/0/1914 Pte Orr Edward W, T/057328 Pte Grant M T/094250 Dr Hurst W T/027037 Pte Rooke W. no change in establishment. Weather fine	OOR
do	7/9		Supplies as on 1st inst. 1 A/D Brvr Shoes AT (No 103) having died struck off the strength. M/Cathrin Fent.	OOR

WAR DIARY
or
INTELLIGENCE SUMMARY.

Army Form C. 2118.

Place	Date	Hour	Summary of Events and Information	Remarks and references to Appendices
KALK	7/4		[illegible handwritten entries]	
		9/4	[illegible handwritten entries]	
		10/4	[illegible handwritten entries]	

Army Form C. 2118.

WAR DIARY
or
INTELLIGENCE SUMMARY.
(Erase heading not required.)

Instructions regarding War Diaries and Intelligence Summaries are contained in F. S. Regs., Part II. and the Staff Manual respectively. Title pages will be prepared in manuscript.

Place	Date	Hour	Summary of Events and Information	Remarks and references to Appendices
Kirkuk	11/9		Supplies as on 1st inst. Weather fine	COR
do	12/9		Supplies as on 1st inst. Weather fine	COR
do	13/9		Supplies drawn from Railhead NEUMAR at 99.15 hours. Weather fine	COR
do	14/9		Arty hy As on Bn inst 7992181 Dr Anson D.B. admitted to No.1 Field Amb. Weather fine	COR
do	15/9		Supplies as on 13th inst. Weather fine	COR
do	16/9		Supplies as on 13th inst. No.201659 Pte Jones J 236 Emp Coy proceeded for duty to attack Sof Hr strength return of unit. Weather fine	COR

Army Form C. 2118.

WAR DIARY
or
INTELLIGENCE SUMMARY.
(Erase heading not required.)

Instructions regarding War Diaries and Intelligence Summaries are contained in F. S. Regs., Part II. and the Staff Manual respectively. Title pages will be prepared in manuscript.

Place	Date	Hour	Summary of Events and Information	Remarks and references to Appendices
KHLK	17/5/19		Supplies as on 12th instant. The following ORs having proceeded to L.H. Abattoir are struck off the strength from unit:- 751/36677 Pte Hill Bertie, 751/37749 L/Cpl Dunn S.H. 751/34932 Pte Cottrell H. Tpr/62263 Pte Balfour F. 706/3211 Pte Batts G. 7/25186 Pte Osborn R. 7/32604 Pte Robinson S. Following Pte Osborn R the following ORs having finished Sergnt's Course in Nai/ub are taken on the strength TS/6606/3 L/Cpl George W. Tr/2204/3 Pte Taylor H. Weather fine.	OSy
do	18/5/19		Supplies as on 13th instant. Weather fine.	OSy
do	19/5/19		Supplies as on 13th instant. The following orders having returned to 23rd Coy from Remounts are taken on the strength of the unit:- No.30169 Pte Pigeon, 70165 Pte Bryan, 20654 Pte Daniels.	OSy

(A9475) Wt W2356/P360 600,000 12/17 D. D. & L. **Sch. 52a.** Forms/C2118/15.

WAR DIARY
or
INTELLIGENCE SUMMARY

Army Form C. 2118.

(Erase heading not required.)

Instructions regarding War Diaries and Intelligence Summaries are contained in F. S. Regs., Part II. and the Staff Manual respectively. Title pages will be prepared in manuscript.

Place	Date	Hour	Summary of Events and Information	Remarks and references to Appendices
K.E.K	20/5		Supplies 60 ex on 13th inst. Weather fine	O.B.M
do	21/5		Supplies 60 ex on 13th inst. 1 A.D. Laret (Nous BY) evacuated to 52nd M.V.S. with 10 inst March SM the strength. No thorns & S.H.S. Transferred from T.H. to Fabien the strength T/7 infan Pr Morey H discharged from Hospital. Weather fine	O.B.M
do	22"		Supplies 60 ex on 13th inst. 1 L/D Lowe (Noad AX) received from D.A.B.C. Taken on the strength Weather fine	O.B.M
do	23"		Supplies 60 ex on 13th inst. No 10226y Pte Drake R being returned to 23rd Remt Coy on 22nd inst for declining struck off the strength. Weather fine	O.B.M

WAR DIARY
INTELLIGENCE SUMMARY

Army Form C. 2118.

Place	Date	Hour	Summary of Events and Information	Remarks and references to Appendices
KALK	24/9		Supplies as on 13th inst. Weather fine	
do	25/9		Supplies as on 13th inst. Weather fine	
do	26/9		Supplies as on 13th inst. The following having proceeded for duty to the 23rd Bn are struck off the strength T/105812 Pte Whyte G. T/058042 Pte Killingworth G. T/02673 Pte Berges T. T/033212 Pte Merritt H. T/343454 Pte Fuller D. The following having passed on the 26th inst from 1st Army Base (M) Coy are taken on the strength T/309227 Pte Vaughan W. T/12632 Pte Thompson J.T. The following having been struck from 23rd Bn but no orders are taken on the strength No 99474 A/Sgt Atkins 40215 Pte Parry 6995 Pte Cole AB. Weather fine	
do	27/9		Supplies as on the 13th inst. The following having arrived from 23rd Bn are taken on strength No 13170 Pte Kendall N0369 Pte Line Coy as orders are taken on the strength. Weather fine	

Army Form C. 2118.

WAR DIARY
or
INTELLIGENCE SUMMARY.
(Erase heading not required.)

Instructions regarding War Diaries and Intelligence Summaries are contained in F. S. Regs., Part II. and the Staff Manual respectively. Title pages will be prepared in manuscript.

Place	Date	Hour	Summary of Events and Information	Remarks and references to Appendices
KALK	28/9		Supplies as on 13th inst. The following having joined on cadres are taken on the strength. No 105621 Pte Merson AJ 131616 Pte Taylor HJ, 137825 Lee JP, 664 83 Pte Poland. T/103761 A/Cpl Hobman. T/103761 A/Cpl Russell CA admitted to 140th Western Field Amb.	CAS
do	29/9		Supplies as on the 13th inst. No 51612 Pte Shot H. having gone from 138 Gurkhas taken on the strength. Weather fine.	Sy
do	30/9		Supplies as on 13th inst. T/103761 A/Cpl Russell A. evacuated to 61 CCS. 4 H.D. & 2 L.D. horses received from DARC on 25 inst taken on the strength. Weather fine.	Sy
do	31/9		Supplies as on 13th inst. No. 10586 Pte Hurley having joined as a baker taken on the strength. 1 H.D. Loose (Class BX) & 2 H.D. (Class A) evacuated to 52 MVS Weather fine.	Sy

Army Form C. 2118.

WAR DIARY
— or —
INTELLIGENCE SUMMARY.
(Erase heading not required.)

Instructions regarding War Diaries and Intelligence Summaries are contained in F. S. Regs., Part II. and the Staff Manual respectively. Title pages will be prepared in manuscript.

Place	Date	Hour	Summary of Events and Information	Remarks and references to Appendices
KKK	1/9		Supplies drawn from Railhead at HEUMAR @ 09.15 hrs Weather fine	M
do	2/9		Supplies as on 1st inst. The following Drivers being Invalided to U.K. for depatn. on 30 May struck off the strength T/10753312 Maren a T/04446b Or Reeder of T/10732309 Parker T/10807242 King T/10807243 [illegible] Or Bradley 26 admitted to hospital whilst on leave U.K. struck off strength as from 27/3/49 T/SR/02137 Cpl. Hoole promoted Sgt. T/05704 L/Cpl. Carrington promoted L/Sgt. 10993 Or Wheeler a applid Full Authority RASC Records No. CR/30/10/CL/19 L/25/49 1 Officer 2/Lieut. J.L. Anger likes RASC evacuated to 52nd MDS on 31st May. G Struck off the strength from that date. Weather fine	M
do	3/9		Willie as on 1st inst. T/0993 Or Leasey transferred to No. 4 Coy T/05692 CQMS Mills rejoined from General Reinforcement Base Depot Recd. transfer from 114 C & taken on strength. Weather fine	M

WAR DIARY
or
INTELLIGENCE SUMMARY.

(Erase heading not required.)

Army Form C. 2118.

Place	Date	Hour	Summary of Events and Information	Remarks and references to Appendices
KAMK	4/9		Supplies as on 1st instl. T0/2/23310 Dr Laws W. admitted 140'F. Clerk Att. M.W. Paget joined on 2nd instl. taken on the strength. Weather fine.	W
do	5/9		Supplies as on 1st instl. Weather fine.	W
do	6/9		Supplies as on 1st instl. Weather fine.	W
do	7/9		Supplies as on 1st instl. T/057566 Dr Wilmot applied T/P.A.L. T/52290 Sgt/Clk Watson applied hary/S/Sgt. T/Mary Mary/Dr Pratt A.b. applied Mary/Sgt. (Authority R.A.S.C Records No. CR/30.78/elis 01/9/19) I.H.D. Lease No. 41 blocks ct erected to 52nd MWS Weather fine	W
do	8/9		Supplies as on 1st instl. Weather fine. T/091338 Dr Patrick R.O. joined from General Reinforcement Depot	W

Army Form C. 2118.

WAR DIARY
— or —
INTELLIGENCE SUMMARY.
(Erase heading not required.)

Instructions regarding War Diaries and Intelligence Summaries are contained in F. S. Regs., Part II. and the Staff Manual respectively. Title pages will be prepared in manuscript.

Place	Date	Hour	Summary of Events and Information	Remarks and references to Appendices
KMLK	9/4/19		The following having proceeded to U.K. for duties are the be [struck] and struck off the strength 739430<s>2</s> Lieut Dr Dale BJ. 734484 Dr Armstrong WJ. 736625. Cpl Dr Read J. 734801 Dr Henry H. 739263. Dr Phelps B. 732887. Dr Watson D. Smith WMG. 732457. Dr Yates J. No. 739340 A/Sgt Watson A transferred to the 3 Coy and from India to Marseilles supplement d/3/10/19. Triple Good/Mgt (4/9/595) Surgeon A.L. awarded M.S.M. Weather fine	M
do	10/6/19		Supplied one Offr and 1 anok. 740946321 Dr Patrick RO for & joined 5th General Reinforcement and Depot is taken on the strength from [illegible]. Weather fine	M

Army Form C. 2118.

WAR DIARY
or
INTELLIGENCE SUMMARY.
(Erase heading not required.)

Instructions regarding War Diaries and Intelligence Summaries are contained in F. S. Regs., Part II. and the Staff Manual respectively. Title pages will be prepared in manuscript.

Place	Date	Hour	Summary of Events and Information	Remarks and references to Appendices
KANTARA	11/9		Supplies as on 1st. No. T/4/108259 Pt. ESSEX.W. admitted hospital	M
			Weather fine.	
	12/9		Supplies as on 1st	
			Weather fine	U
	13/9		Supplies as on 1st. The undermentioned proceeded to Geneva for 13.9.19 and are struck off strength.	M
			T/4/62/140 Sgt. SCOTT. W.P. T/393615 Cpl. WHITE.D. T/89229 Cpl. Cox.H. T/11399 Pt. BULLEY C.A.J. T/0456/ Pt. CRANE.W. T/0601 Pt. CLEAR.J. T/1/1023 Pt. LUCAS S.H.	
			Weather fine	
	14/9		Supplies as on 1st. No. T/4/24/261 Pt. HAINES. A.E. proceeded from 30 Cavalry Reserve Park.	M
			Weather fine	
	15/9		Supplies as on 1st. No. T/4/108250 Pt. ESSEX.W. discharged from hospital to dy at Kantara.	M
			Weather fine.	

(19175) Wt. W3355/P360 600,000 12/17 D.D. & L. Sch. 52a. Forms/C2118/15.

WAR DIARY
or
INTELLIGENCE SUMMARY.
(Erase heading not required.)

Army Form C. 2118.

Place	Date	Hour	Summary of Events and Information	Remarks and references to Appendices
KANTARA	15/9		Supplies as on 1st. 19 horse Nostri (Cx) evacuated to 2gus NZMS on 13th. Struck off strength. Weather fine	M
"	14/9		Supplies to fill 1st. 10 horses H.Q. Chillong Pl admitted to field hospital. Weather fine	M
"	15/9		Supplies as on 1st. No 17626155 Dr Schofield L Joined from 1st Army Aux (H) Coy	M
"	18/9		Supplies as on 1st.	M
"	19/9		Supplies as on 1st. Weather fine	M
"	20/9		Supplies as on 1st. Weather fine	M
"	21/9		Supplies as on 1st. Weather fine	M

Army Form C. 2118.

WAR DIARY
or
INTELLIGENCE SUMMARY.
(Erase heading not required.)

Instructions regarding War Diaries and Intelligence Summaries are contained in F. S. Regs., Part II. and the Staff Manual respectively. Title pages will be prepared in manuscript.

Place	Date	Hour	Summary of Events and Information	Remarks and references to Appendices
Ralk	22/9		Supplies as on 1st. The undermentioned proceeded to hospital sick two on 29th and one on 30th from that date.	
			763105 Pt. Briggs C.E.; 43634 Pt. Cuddings A.; 43636 Pt. Collins G.C.;	
			704145 Pt. Crocker E.; 458169 Pt. Davis E.H.; 40689 Pt. Essex W.;	
			74881 Pt. Goodwin A.; 44104 Pt. Herring W.; 70419 Pt. Hiron P.;	M
			74856 Pt. Holland D.; 74041 Pt. Holey J.; 74724 Pt. Harvey C.;	
			74220 Pt. Mosser W.; 40535 Pt. Mallether; 43855 Cpl. Osborne T.S.;	
			74532 Pt. Powell J.; 40529 Pt. Whiteside W.; 40448 Pt. Watkins S.J.;	
			102140 Pt. Watson W.R.; 43854 Pt. Walker J.	
			Weather fine	M
	23/9		Supplies as on 1st. Weather fine	M
	24/9		Supplies as on 1st. Weather wet	M
	25/9		Supplies as on 1st. Weather wet	M

Army Form C. 2118.

WAR DIARY
or
INTELLIGENCE SUMMARY.
(Erase heading not required.)

Instructions regarding War Diaries and Intelligence Summaries are contained in F. S. Regs., Part II. and the Staff Manual respectively. Title pages will be prepared in manuscript.

Place	Date	Hour	Summary of Events and Information	Remarks and references to Appendices
Ka UK	26/6/19		Supplies as on 1st. Weather fine	
			T/405,586 Dr WILSON F. appointed MOd 8/6/19 assumed duty with Bde 21/6/19 (Authy RAS.C. Records MOCR/301/8/4/16 d/5/29)	M
"	27/6/19		Supplies as on 1st. Weather fine	M
"	28/6/19		Supplies as on 1st Weather fine	
			T/04544 Dr. BLYTHING O discharged from No.6 General Hospital & taken on the strength 24-6-19. T/4/213310 Dr POW W admitted to hospital 28-6-19.	M
"	29/6/19		Supplies as on 1st PEACE SIGNED Weather fine	M
			Dr T/404254 Dr Patrick R O & T/3658 Dr Wilson G admitted to 164th C.C.S. 29/7/9 the undermentioned wounded to Depot 27/7/79	
			SS/1120 Cpl Whyte J. T/343367 Dr Haines R.E.W. T/14677 Dr Deary M. T/049193 Dr Elliott R. T/261523 Dr 10th C.M. T/26915 Mule O. T/102113 Cpl Lunn RE T/212207 Cpl Kendall SK, Ty 233219 Pte Ayres H	M

(A9175) Wt W4358/P366 600,000 12/17 D.D. & L. Sch. 52a. Forms/C2118/5.

Army Form C. 2118.

WAR DIARY
or
INTELLIGENCE SUMMARY.
(Erase heading not required.)

Instructions regarding War Diaries and Intelligence Summaries are contained in F. S. Regs., Part II. and the Staff Manual respectively. Title pages will be prepared in manuscript.

Place	Date	Hour	Summary of Events and Information	Remarks and references to Appendices
Kalk	30/6/18		Supplies as on 1st	Weather fine W
Kalk	1st July 1918			

Adam
Major
O.C. No 1. Coy, Kaba Dist. Siam

WAR DIARY
or
INTELLIGENCE SUMMARY.
(Erase heading not required.)

Army Form C. 2118.

Place	Date	Hour	Summary of Events and Information	Remarks and references to Appendices
H.O.K	1/9		Surplus drawn from Railhead at Heenan at 09.15hrs	VI
			Weather fine	
R.O.K	2/9		Surplus as on 1st	
			Pvt C.J Blindnatt R.A.S.C. admitted 36 C.C.S. 1/9	
			T4/146492 Pt Davies O.H sick. confined from 52nd M.V.S. 2/9	
			T3/25929 Pt Cooney O. transfered to 52nd M.V.S. 2/9	VI
R.O.K	3/9		Surplus as on 1st	VI
R.O.K	4/9		Surplus as on 1st	
			Weather fine	
			The unmanufactured N.C.O's. men, vehicles & Lorries Trailers &c left during duty tin on return of the strength with it	
			Unit from H 4/9 — T3/8960 Sgb. Dr Travers S, T4/211224	
			S.I.R CK Woberry, £ 11/9; T3/17677 M.K Pr. Peebbles T/. W.C	
			T4/238643 M.K G.S Luff S.L.; T3/146072 Pm. Davies O.H	VI

WAR DIARY
or
INTELLIGENCE SUMMARY.

Army Form C. 2118.

Place	Date	Hour	Summary of Events and Information	Remarks and references to Appendices
Kalk	5/7/19		Supplies as on 1st. Weather fine.	M
Kalk	6/7/19		Supplies as on 1st. Weather wet.	M
Kalk	7/7/19		Supplies as on 1st. Weather fine. 1st 601 Sn S/Sgt Brodie R. proceeded on leave to U.K. Recd Blacksmith C/M transferred to 3rd General Hospital 7/19. 15/369 Wh/y B.Sgt. in H.Q.B. proba to No 11 Coy R.A.S.C. Jordan. Diarrhoea cases 7-7-19.	M
Kalk	8/7/19		Supplies as on 1st. weather wet	M
Kalk	9/7/19		Supplies as on 1st. 7/35677 Sc. Highley A.G. refused for Convalescent Depôt. Undertaken 9/7/19. Weather fine.	M

WAR DIARY
or
INTELLIGENCE SUMMARY.
(Erase heading not required.)

Army Form C. 2118.

Place	Date	Hour	Summary of Events and Information	Remarks and references to Appendices
K de K	10/6 /19		Surplus as on 1st. Weather fine.	
			T4/R1 Cpl Edwards S.E. to be Cpl 14.7.19 Assumes duty with pay	
			8.7.19 vice T0 T4/094219 Cpl Cox A. demobilized 13-6-19.	
			S4/044579 Pte Bosworth G to be Cpl Issues 14.7.19 Assumes duty	
			with pay 8.7.19 vice T4/516627 Cpl Clark Q demobilized 13-6-19	
			T4/104934 L/Cpl Chitland A. to be Cpl L 10.7.19 Assumes duty with pay	
			8-7-19 vice T4/SR/0554 L/Cpl Yates E.S. promoted to Sgt A.S	
			T4/094085 Pte Gray H. to be L/Cpl 21.7.19 Assumes duty with Pay	
			8-7-19 vice T4/107185 L/Cpl Osborne W.C demobilized 20.6.19	
			T4/094239 Pte Forde C. to be L/Cpl 14.7.19 Assumes duty with pay	
			8.7.19 vice T4 T3/024493 L/Cpl Brennan to demobilized 13-6-19.	
			T3/54725 Pte Harding A.J. to be A/L/Cpl 11.5.19. Assumes duty with	
			pay 1-7-19. vice T4/107195 L/Cpl Chitland A. promoted to Cpl 10.5.19	
			T5/M241 Wkr L/Cpl Pratt A.E.H. with SS 9.10.S.S Assumes duty with	
			pay 2-7-19. vice T6 T5/M39 Wkr S/Sgt Harriott E.G demobilized 9-5-19	
			Authy RASO. A. Records 11e CR/SAA/OP/142 dated 30/6/19.	

Army Form C. 2118.

WAR DIARY
or
INTELLIGENCE SUMMARY.
(Erase heading not required.)

Instructions regarding War Diaries and Intelligence Summaries are contained in F. S. Regs., Part II. and the Staff Manual respectively. Title pages will be prepared in manuscript.

Place	Date	Hour	Summary of Events and Information	Remarks and references to Appendices
RolK	11/1/19		Supplies as on 1st. Weather fine. 7/36 &4/45 Pte McSham M awarded 1st G.C. Badge 10/7/19	M.
RolK	12/7/19		Supplies as on 1st. Weather wet	M.
RolK	13/7/19		Supplies as on 1st. Weather fair	M.
RolK	14/7/19		Supplies as on 1st. 75/7672 WhrS Sgt Parsons O posted to No 4 Coy 14/7/19 75/7614 Pratt A E posted from No 4 Coy 14/7/19 -do- Weather fine	M.
RolK	15/7/19		Supplies as on 1st. Weather fine. Shir Road held at No 1 Coy Rendez. Dist. Jump. Lt M. Dunhope i/c testing men as Shoeing Smiths Asst. President Major A. Sadler DSO RASC	M.

Army Form C. 2118.

WAR DIARY
or
INTELLIGENCE SUMMARY.
(Erase heading not required.)

Instructions regarding War Diaries and Intelligence Summaries are contained in F. S. Regs., Part II. and the Staff Manual respectively. Title pages will be prepared in manuscript.

Place	Date	Hour	Summary of Events and Information	Remarks and references to Appendices
Kalk	16/4/19		Supplies as on 1st	Weather fine
Kalk	17/4/19		Supplies as on 1st	Weather fine
Kalk	18/4/19		Supplies as on 1st	Weather showery
Kalk	19/4/19		Supplies as on 1st	Weather wet
Kalk	20/4/19		Supplies as on 1st	Weather fine
Kalk	21/4/19		Supplies as on 1st	Weather fine
Kalk	22/4/19		Supplies as on 1st. Court of Enquiry assembling at No 3 Coy Office to investigate illegal absence of 7/68375 Pte Powell V.B.	Weather fine

Army Form C. 2118.

WAR DIARY
or
INTELLIGENCE SUMMARY.
(Erase heading not required.)

Instructions regarding War Diaries and Intelligence Summaries are contained in F. S. Regs., Part II. and the Staff Manual respectively. Title pages will be prepared in manuscript.

Place	Date	Hour	Summary of Events and Information	Remarks and references to Appendices
Kalk	23/7/19		Supplies as on 1st	Weather wet
Kalk	24/7/19		Supplies as on 1st	Weather showery
Kalk	25/7/19		Supplies as on 1st	Weather fine
Kalk	26/7/19		Supplies as on 1st. T4/185714 Pte Rhodes JC & T5/8483 Pr Dr Lodd W proceeded to UK (ex Demoth. 26.7.19) are struck off strength from that date	Weather fine
Kalk	27/7/19		Supplies as on 1st	Weather wet
Kalk	28/7/19		Supplies as on 1st	Weather fine

Army Form C. 2118.

WAR DIARY
or
INTELLIGENCE SUMMARY.

(Erase heading not required.)

Instructions regarding War Diaries and Intelligence Summaries are contained in F. S. Regs., Part II. and the Staff Manual respectively. Title pages will be prepared in manuscript.

Place	Date	Hour	Summary of Events and Information	Remarks and references to Appendices
Kalk	29/9/19		Supplies as on 1st	Weather wet
Kalk	30/9/19		Supplies as on 1st	Weather fine
Kalk	31/9/19		Supplies as on 1st	Weather fine

Kalk 15/1/19

Adam Major
O.C. 16 Coy London Surplus Train

WAR DIARY
or
INTELLIGENCE SUMMARY.
(Erase heading not required.)

Army Form C. 2118.

Place	Date	Hour	Summary of Events and Information	Remarks and references to Appendices
Koull	1/8/19		Supplies drawn from Redhead at Herman at 09.15 hours	hours
	2/8/19		Supplies as on 1st. Weather fine. Machinery parts & the undermentioned men having been transferred from 13th Field Ambulance are taken on the strength with effect from 1st August /19. T/19.0002 Pte O'Neill E, T/237263 Pte J Thomas Pte Payne W, T/457509 Pte Reich, T/324413 Pte Stewart, T Thomas & Pte Hanson DC	
	3/8/19		Supplies as on 1st. Weather dull & fine	
	4/8/19		Supplies as on 1st. T/2568? Pte Hughes W. proceeded to U.K. for demob 4/8/19. Weather fine	

Army Form C. 2118.

WAR DIARY
or
INTELLIGENCE SUMMARY.
(Erase heading not required.)

Instructions regarding War Diaries and Intelligence Summaries are contained in F. S. Regs., Part II. and the Staff Manual respectively. Title pages will be prepared in manuscript.

Place	Date	Hour	Summary of Events and Information	Remarks and references to Appendices
Rathly	5/7/19		Supplies as on 1st	Weather fine MWP
	6/7/19		Supplies as on 1st T/24125 S/K Cpl Cowell J.T.S. att'd 4th A.Sqdn S.Sgts 5-7-19 free T/5/8/90 S/K Sgt Woodward A.E. demobilged 5-7-19 Assumes duty with pay 3-7-19 T/24125 S/Sgt & S/Sgt Cowell J.T.S. transferred to No 2 Coy London Dist Train 4/7/19	Weather fine MWP
	7/7/19		Supplies as on 1st	Weather dull MWP
	8/7/19		Supplies as on 1st T/453395 Dvr Millhouse J.R. T/453395 Dvr Pennington W admitted to Field Amb 7-8-19	Weather fair MWP
	9/7/19		Supplies as on 1st	Weather wet MWP

WAR DIARY
or
INTELLIGENCE SUMMARY

Army Form C. 2118.

Place	Date	Hour	Summary of Events and Information	Remarks and references to Appendices
KJR	10/9		Supplies as on 1st. Weather fair	A/119
			T/37611 Cpl Russell A.R. discharged to Gen¹ Hosp. 6-8-19	
	11/9		Supplies as on 1st. Weather fine	A/119
			T/453405 Pte Milliquet L.K. discharged 139ᵗʰ Field Amb 10-7-19	
	12/9		Supplies as on 1st. Weather fine	A/119
	13/9		Supplies as on 1st. Weather dull	A/119
	14/9		Supplies as on 1st. Weather wet	A/119
	15/9		Supplies as on 1st. Weather fine	A/119
			S/4334/6 Pte Harding E. O. discharged 139ᵗʰ Field Amb 15/9/9	
	16/9		Supplies as on 1st. Weather fair	A/119
			T4/051491 O.S.M. Riley P.S. posted to 139ᵗʰ Field Amb 15-8-19	

Army Form C. 2118.

WAR DIARY
or
INTELLIGENCE SUMMARY.
(Erase heading not required.)

Instructions regarding War Diaries and Intelligence Summaries are contained in F. S. Regs., Part II. and the Staff Manual respectively. Title pages will be prepared in manuscript.

Place	Date	Hour	Summary of Events and Information	Remarks and references to Appendices
Depot Kalk	17/8/19		Supplies as on 1st	Weather fine 6/8/19
Kalk	18/8/19		Supplies as on 1st. T/105995 Pte Chetland A discharged K2 "Stationary Hosp" 17-8-19	Weather fine 6/8/19
Kalk	19/8/19		Supplies as on 1st	Weather fine 6/8/19
Kalk	20/8/19		Supplies as on 1st	Weather fine 6/8/19
Kalk	21/8/19		Supplies as on 1st. T/454034 Sgt L.H. Marsden A/S to A/CQMS vice T/62998 CQMS L.M. Mills W. demobilized 28/6/19. Assumes duty with Day 21-8-19. T/010101 Cpl Burmaster E a/n/w A/Sgt vice T/419372 Sgt Scott H.O.P. demobilized 13-6-19. Assumes duty with Day 21-8-19.	Weather wet 6/8/19

WAR DIARY
or
INTELLIGENCE SUMMARY.

(Erase heading not required.)

Army Form C. 2118.

Instructions regarding War Diaries and Intelligence Summaries are contained in F. S. Regs., Part II. and the Staff Manual respectively. Title pages will be prepared in manuscript.

Place	Date	Hour	Summary of Events and Information	Remarks and references to Appendices
Kalk	22/7/19		Supplies as on 1st	Weather fine
Kalk	23/7/19		Supplies as on 1st. T/2135/10 Pte Post W. discharged 25th General Hospital 22-7-19.	Weather wet
Kalk	24/7/19		Supplies as on 1st	Weather fine
Kalk	25/7/19		Supplies as on 1st	Weather fine
Kalk	26/7/19		Supplies as on 1st	Weather dull
Kalk	27/7/19		Supplies as on 1st	Weather fine
Kalk	28/7/19		Supplies as on 1st	Weather wet

Army Form C. 2118.

WAR DIARY
or
INTELLIGENCE SUMMARY.
(Erase heading not required.)

Place	Date	Hour	Summary of Events and Information	Remarks and references to Appendices
Kalk	29/7		Supplies as on 1st. Weather fine	6/W/D
Kalk	30/7		Supplies as on 1st. Weather wet	6/W/D
Kalk	31/7		Supplies as on 1st. Weather fine. T/040835 Sgt. Ross C. att. to A/C.Q.M. (W.O.Class II) W.19 new No. T/196841 C.S.M. Seacroft demobilized 4-7-19. Absumes duty with pay 31-8-19.	6/W/D

Kalk 31-7-19.

O.C. 16 (Coy) London Division
A/J.G. Bagot Lieut

Army Form C. 2118.

WAR DIARY
or
INTELLIGENCE SUMMARY.
(Erase heading not required.)

Place	Date	Hour	Summary of Events and Information	Remarks and references to Appendices
Kalk	1/9/19		Supplies drawn from Railhead at 09.00 hours. T/185105 Pte Dawson H.A., T/265158 Dr Schofield h., T/269975 Dr Taylor W.H., having proceeded to U.K. for demobilization 31/8/19 are struck off the strength from that date. T/053460 Dr Larkin A.C. admitted 13 of F.A. 19.	Weather fine. W
Kalk	2/9/19		Supplies as on 1st	Weather fine. W
Kalk	3/9/19		Supplies as on 1st. T/053392 Dr Dowling A.W. granted leave to U.K. 3/9/19 to 16/9/19.	Weather dull. W
Kalk	4/9/19		Supplies as on 1st	Weather fine. W
Kalk	5/9/19		Supplies as on 1st. T/12121 Dr Mutherdill Y.W., T/4533 93 Dr Rudge A., & T/45337 Pte. Gerard K.C. granted leave to U.K. 5/9/19 to 19/9/19.	Weather wet. W
Kalk	6/9/19		Supplies as on 1st	Weather fine. W

Army Form C. 2118.

WAR DIARY
or
INTELLIGENCE SUMMARY.
(Erase heading not required.)

Instructions regarding War Diaries and Intelligence Summaries are contained in F. S. Regs., Part II. and the Staff Manual respectively. Title pages will be prepared in manuscript.

Place	Date	Hour	Summary of Events and Information	Remarks and references to Appendices
Kalk	7/9/19		Supplies as on 1st. Weather fine	A
Kalk	8/9/19		Supplies as on 1st. Weather dull. T/SR.02139 Sgt Hatch G.E posted to No 3 Coy. Laden Burgen 8-9. T/Oquilet Dr William W admitted 139th Field Amb. 8-9-19.	A
Kalk	9/9/19		Supplies as on 1st. Weather fine. T/453482 Dr Barnett W.E; T/45307 Dr Lyatt G.; T/453494 Dr Hill B Sgt T/453469 Dr Sargent A.B. posted & taken on the strength from 10 Sqd Laden B.J. 9-9-19.	A
Kalk	10/9/19		Supplies as on 1st. Weather fine. T/453400 Dr Lonkin H.C. discharged 139th F.A. 10-9-19.	A
Kalk	11/9/19		Supplies as on 1st. Weather fine. T/453507 Dr Lyatt G admitted 140th F.A. 10.9. T/453380 Dr Jolly H. admitted 140th F.A. 11-9-19	A
Kalk	12/9/19		Supplies as on 1st. Weather wet. T/453482 Dr Barnett W.E. admitted 140th F.A 12/9/19.	A

Army Form C. 2118.

WAR DIARY
or
INTELLIGENCE SUMMARY.
(Erase heading not required.)

Instructions regarding War Diaries and Intelligence Summaries are contained in F. S. Regs., Part II. and the Staff Manual respectively. Title pages will be prepared in manuscript.

Place	Date	Hour	Summary of Events and Information	Remarks and references to Appendices
Kalk	13/9/19		Supplies as on 1st. Weather fine. T/0996. Dr Williams W. admitted discharged 139th F.A. 13-9-19	M
Kalk	14/9/19		Supplies as on 1st. Weather fine	M
Kalk	15/9/19		Supplies as on 1st. Weather dull	M
Kalk	16/9/19		Supplies as on 1st. Weather fine	M
Kalk	17/9/19		Supplies as on 1st. T/45380 Dr Trollope L.A. discharged 140th F.A. 17-9-19. Weather wet	M
Kalk	18/9/19		Supplies as on 1st. T/45407 Dr Wyatt G. discharged 140th F.A. 18-9-19. Weather wet	M
Kalk	19/9/19		Supplies as on 1st. Weather fine	M
Kalk	20/9/19		Supplies as on 1st. Weather fine	M
Kalk	21/9/19		Supplies as on 1st. Weather wet	M

Army Form C. 2118.

WAR DIARY
or
INTELLIGENCE SUMMARY.
(Erase heading not required.)

Instructions regarding War Diaries and Intelligence Summaries are contained in F. S. Regs., Part II. and the Staff Manual respectively. Title pages will be prepared in manuscript.

Place	Date	Hour	Summary of Events and Information	Remarks and references to Appendices
Kalk	22/9/19		Supplies as on 1st. T/145/351 Pte Bridge W + T/145/407 Pte Ransom P. granted 6 bt. Rate of Corps Pay with effect from 20-9-19. Weather fine	M
Kalk	23/9/19		Supplies as on 1st. Weather wet	M
Kalk	24/9/19		Supplies as on 1st. T/153298 Pte Petty J. granted leave to U.K. 24-9-19 to 8-19-19. Weather fine	M
Kalk	25/9/19		Supplies as on 1st. T/145/326 Pte Gaff J.R admitted 140th F.A. 25-9-19. Weather fine	M
Kalk	26/9/19		Supplies as on 1st. Weather dull	M
Kalk	27/9/19		Supplies as on 1st. T/294249 Pte Morrison D.S., T/040835 C.S.M. Low C + T/145735, Pte Bridges W. granted leave to U.K. from 27-9-19 to 11-10-19. Weather fine	M
Kalk	28/9/19		Supplies as on 1st. Weather wet	M

Army Form C. 2118.

WAR DIARY
or
INTELLIGENCE SUMMARY.

(Erase heading not required.)

Instructions regarding War Diaries and Intelligence Summaries are contained in F. S. Regs., Part II. and the Staff Manual respectively. Title pages will be prepared in manuscript.

Place	Date	Hour	Summary of Events and Information	Remarks and references to Appendices
Kalk	29/9/19		Supplies as on 1st.	Weather Fine.
Kalk	30/9/19		Supplies as on 1st.	Weather Fine.

[signature] Major
O.C. No 1 Coy, Ranche Div. Train

30 Sept/1919.

NO. 1 COMPANY.
DIVISIONAL TRAIN.

www.ingramcontent.com/pod-product-compliance
Lightning Source LLC
Chambersburg PA
CBHW082007220426
43670CB00014B/2570